Withdrawn from stock

University College Cork

Villages in the Landscape

Archaeology in the Field Series

Villages in the Landscape

Trevor Rowley

J. M. Dent & Sons Ltd
London   Toronto   Melbourne

First published 1978
© Trevor Rowley 1978

Printed in Great Britain at
Biddles Ltd, Guildford, for
J. M. Dent & Sons Ltd
Aldine House, Albemarle Street, London

This book is set in 11 on 12 pt VIP Bembo

British Library Cataloguing in Publication Data

Rowley, Trevor
    Villages in the landscape. – (Archaeology
    in the field series).
    1. Villages – England – History
    I. Title   II. Series
    942'.00973'4   DA115

    ISBN 0-460-04166-5

Contents

List of Plates

Villages in the landscape

Preface

Hundreds of individual parish and village histories have been written over the past century or so, yet no attempt has ever been made to write the definitive story of the English village. It was not until I started work on this book that I began to appreciate the reason for this. Each parish, village and hamlet has its own unique story and any attempt to blend them into a coherent narrative is fraught with difficulty. The subject matter by its very nature demands a multi-disciplinary approach – geographical, historical, archaeological and even sociological. When this approach is applied to such a nebulous concept as the 'village', the difficulties increase enormously. Nevertheless, given that our ability to change our environment rapidly has never been greater, there is a desire and a need to understand and conserve the landscape of rural settlement, past and present. With some humility, therefore, I present some ideas on how the topic might be examined in the hope that it will stimulate others to question and understand our villages more fully.

Reluctantly I have used the post-1974 administrative counties, although historically these are of course nonsensical. All the village plans used are based on the first edition Ordnance Survey twenty-five inch and six inch maps unless stated otherwise, these have the advantage not only of being out of copyright but also of depicting village England, just before it was changed out of all recognition by the arrival of the motor car.

For the sake of convenience the traditional archaeological three-stage system is used throughout the book; the terminology should, however, be treated with great caution and must

11

not be taken literally. The terms are used to give some idea of general chronology in the absence of specific dating evidence from many sites. The attribution of a site or village to a particular period should also be treated with some care, as there is mounting evidence to indicate that rigid dating boundaries are relatively meaningless.

Trevor Rowley
Hethe, Oxfordshire
February 1978

Acknowledgments

Thanks are due to many people who have helped with the creation of this book. In particular I would like to thank Michael Aston, David Miles and Christopher Taylor for their comments and advice; any errors or misconceptions are, however, solely mine. I would also like to thank Lisa Brown and Alison Smith for the production of the plans, Linda Rowley, Sylvia Pryor, Shirley Hermon and the secretarial staff of Rewley House for the typing and checking of the text and the indexing.

I am also grateful to the following for permission to redraw their published plans: Barry Cuncliffe, figs 2 and 12; George Jobey, fig. 15; Peter Wade-Martins, fig. 18; Charles Johnson, fig. 19; John Hurst, fig. 22; Hugh Clout, fig. 30; James Bond, figs 32, 34 and 36; Anne Ellison, fig. 37 and the Cambridge University Committee for Aerial Photography for permission to reproduce plates 2, 3, 25, 23, 20, 9, 5, 14, 4, 10, 26, 12, 21, 13; Aerofilms for plates, 1, 6, 8, 17, 18 and 22; the National Monuments Record for plate 7; the Oxfordshire Archaeological Committee for plate 11; Peter Addyman for plate 16 and to the Committee for Rescue Archaeology in Gloucester, Avon and Somerset for permission to reproduce the survey of Isle Abbots as Appendix 1.

1 Villages in the landscape

It has been estimated that there are well over ten thousand villages in Britain. At the time of the first national census in 1801, over three-quarters of the population of England and Wales lived outside towns, principally in hamlets and villages. By 1971 well under a quarter of the population could be thought of as rural inhabitants. Thus in under two centuries we have changed from being a predominantly rural to a pre-dominantly urban society. It is true that this change has taken place against a massive increase in the overall population, and that the actual number of people living outside strictly urban areas has increased from roughly six-and-a-half million in 1801 to just over ten million in 1971. Nevertheless, at the beginning of the nineteenth century the majority of people lived in villages and worked close to where they lived, most of them in agriculture. Today under 3 per cent of the population works on the land and the majority of village dwellers earn their living away from their home settlement.

There is a tendency to think of country life as stable, conservative and unchanging but this is far from the truth. Settlements, like the men who live in them, are mortal. There is, however, no recognizable expected life-span, and a village can survive for twenty or two thousand years depending on its ability to adapt to changing economic and social conditions. In addition to extant village communities there are in Britain thousands of former occupation sites which have been abandoned. Some, particularly those deserted recently, have left obvious traces in the form of ruined buildings or earthworks, some have been eroded over the centuries and are visible only from the air as cropmarks, while others have been built over, quarried away or have simply disappeared leaving no surviving traces.

Rural settlement in the past reflected the ever-changing relationship between man and his environment. Human society is never completely static and the settlements which serve it can never remain absolutely still for very long; and before a well-balanced form of settlement becomes generally established, new forces will be at work subtly altering that form. There is therefore no simple chronological sequence of settlement history, no inevitable progression of rural settlement, from small to large, simple to complex, from irregular to regular. We are dealing with an immensely complicated and delicately balanced organism. The forces which created our hamlets and villages have involved factors as varied as the pace of technological development, the nature of local authority, inheritance customs, the presence of arable or pasture, and the availability of building material. Village history tells a story of fluctuating expansion, decline and movement. Sometimes reflecting national factors such as pestilence, economic change and social development and sometimes purely local events, such as the silting up of a river estuary or the bankruptcy of a local entrepreneur. Such factors have combined to give each village a unique history and plan.

The complexity of the details of rural settlement history in Britain has only really been appreciated in recent years through the development of local historical and landscape studies. Patterns of settlement and place-names as they appear on nineteenth- and twentieth-century maps have been taken very much at their face value by geographers and historians alike in the past. We must now accept that at any one time settlement geography will be changing, and often changing in different ways, both locally and regionally. We must be equally wary about accepting purely ethnic or geological explanations for patterns and forms of settlement, for although they may have played some role in fashioning village morphology, they are simply two ingredients out of many.

The picture is a complicated one because settlements are organic: single farmsteads can be joined together over the years to form a community, or conversely a village can fragment into isolated settlements. Often such changes will take place within a fossilized administrative framework, for instance, many parishes survived for centuries after the community they originally served had dispersed or even disappeared, and in medieval documents a place-name of a former village may be applied to a group of isolated farmsteads for the sake of administrative convenience.

The study of settlements and settlement patterns involves extremely complicated interrelationships. A village will evolve or be created as a result of a particular combination of geographical, commercial, economic, social and political factors. As one or more of these change, the village structure will respond, both socially and morphologically, and this may result in the stagnation, growth, decline or abandonment of the settlement. Normally once established there are strong reasons to preserve the site and form of the settlement, but in many cases other influences will override this inertia, and these will be reflected in changes both in the physical and economic structure of the community.

A major element is the willingness or otherwise of the land owner or owners (in some literature called the 'dominant authority') in the community to initiate or tolerate change. In the twentieth century it is principally local government and individual land owners, not the village community, that have this power. In the past it was mainly the manorial lord or freehold farmers who were responsible for initiating changes in the village. Fossilization is a factor in the control of the dominant authority; for example many estate villages are commonly called 'closed' as opposed to 'open' villages where no obvious control was exercised. Such fossilization may have been a conscious or unconscious decision. Even where there was a great deal of flexibility within a community there would have been some fossilization, for instance, in the roads or tenement boundaries. The physical appearance of the village will reflect both change and stagnation. It is the task of the landscape historian to identify these features, to place them in some sort of chronological order, to interpret the factors which led to their creation in the first place, and then to account for their whole or partial survival.

Villages in the landscape

The analysis of villages requires that a distinction be made between the pattern of rural settlement and the morphology of individual rural communities. Both will vary historically and geographically, but it is easier to generalize with confidence about the former. One of the first English scholars, F. W. Maitland, who tried to understand the historical development of rural settlement, grappled with this problem. In his great work *Domesday Book and Beyond* (1897) he reproduced two portions of the first edition one inch Ordnance Survey map to demonstrate a dramatic contrast between a land of nucleated villages in Oxfordshire and Berkshire and a land of hamlets in Somerset and Devon. In the village proper he explained: 'here is only one cluster of houses. It is a fairly large cluster; it stands in the midst of its fields, of its territory, and until lately a considerable part of its territory will probably have consisted of spacious "common fields" '; on the other hand in the land of hamlets 'the houses which lie within the boundary of the parish are scattered about in small clusters; here two or three, there three or four. These clusters often have names of their own, and it seems mere chance that the name worn by one of them should also be the name of the whole parish.'

Rural settlement, therefore, varies not only in time but also in space, although until about 1800 a national pattern could be identified. Houses and farm buildings clustered around village greens, abutted onto village streets, stood close to churches, castles, bridges or harbours. Small nucleated communities predominated in a zone from Northumberland to Devon. Despite fundamental agrarian and industrial developments since the Middle Ages the village had survived as the basic form of settlement in Britain. Because the speed of communication and movement of people and produce was largely unchanged a considerable proportion of the nucleated villages that had evolved to accommodate open-field agriculture in the Middle Ages had remained in existence, albeit often in a radically altered form. Over most of the Midlands from the Pennines to the Chilterns it was still somewhat unusual to see a farm or cottage outside a village until the nineteenth century. Westwards from the Cotswolds towards Devon and the Welsh Marches the villages became smaller, more irregular in

18

arrangement and hamlets appeared more frequently. Devonshire and Herefordshire were mainly counties of hamlets, consisting of groups of three or four farmhouses and cottages, some with an inn or blacksmith and some elevated by the presence of a church. The villages in the West Country were surrounded by dispersed hamlets and isolated farms, and the degree of dispersion increased west of the River Exe. In west Cornwall the only nucleated rural settlements were fishing villages, and mining centres. Throughout the kingdom there were regional variations reflecting local geographical, economic and commercial circumstances.

Over the past two centuries, particularly since 1850, this pattern has been considerably modified over much of Britain. In the Midlands and the north-east, industrial communities have grown up on coalfields and ironstone outcrops. Over much of England new hamlets have been stimulated and old settlements retarded by the coming of the canal, railway, and more recently, roads. The rationalization of agriculture has continued to take its toll of rural communities and those sited away from towns continue to decline. Conversely many villages have been sucked into ever-expanding urban sprawls, and those lying within 20 kilometres of employment centres have been expanded to act as 'dormitories' for commuters.

The most profound change has been sociological. Today village communities are largely divorced from their immediate environment, and the majority of apparently thriving rural settlements are merely an extension of cities, resulting from the development of the commuter train and the private motor car. Today there is no basic difference between town and country life in that the inhabitants of both share or aspire to a common style and standard of living based on international mass marketing. Those picturesque conservation-conscious villages that have survived apparently untouched by the twentieth century are antiques in that they are irreplaceable, suitable for the commuter, the retired and the tourist. The fundamental change of status and of function makes the definition of 'village' very difficult. Most of the criteria which in the past could have been applied to defining a village are today inappropriate. For the purpose of this discussion we shall, therefore, have to largely exclude the twentieth-century suburban village communities and concentrate on those surviving physical aspects of villages which were established at a time when those criteria had some meaning.

We all have a favourite idea of a village with its church, manor house, inn, smithy, a scatter of picturesque thatched cottages and the village stores. This caricature is well expressed by Miss Mitford in *Our Village* (1824):

> Of all situations for constant residence, that which appeals to me most delightful is a little village far in the country; a small neighbourhood, not of fine mansions finely peopled but of cottages and cottage-like houses, 'messuages or tenements', as a friend of mine calls such ignoble and non-descript dwellings, with inhabitants whose faces are familiar to us as the flowers in our garden; a little world of our own, close packed and insulated like ants in an ant hill, or bees in a hive, or sheep in a fold, or nuns in a convent, or sailors in a ship; where we know everyone, are known to everyone, interested in everyone, and authority to hope that everyone feels an interest in us.

This conventional if somewhat patronizing portrait does contain elements of truth, in that it depicts a relatively self-contained and self-sufficient rural community.

The basic problem of definition is that, 'village' has no tenurial or legal significance. Strictly speaking the term 'village' comes from the Latin word *villaticus* meaning 'an assemblage of houses outside or pertaining to a villa'. In geographical terms a village has been defined as a 'nucleated rural settlement of twenty or more homesteads, a large village being distinguishable from a small market town by its paucity of services'. A hamlet on the other hand is taken to be 'a nucleated settlement, with or without a parish church having from three to nineteen houses'. The term village is also normally applied to that settlement in the parish where the church is sited; if there is no parish church then the settlement, however large, and whatever functions it performs, notionally at least remains a hamlet.

Our twentieth-century commuter village is dramatically different from the medieval village, and would be quite unrecognizable to the people who lived in prehistoric nucleated settlements, and yet these communities both past and present are covered under the heading 'village'. For our purposes the village will cover rural communities which are or have been dependent to some extent upon local resources, whether agrarian, industrial or commercial. Before the invention of the internal combustion engine the majority of the inhabitants of a village would have earned their living from within their own territory; in the Middle Ages this territory was the manor, in earlier times it may have been an estate or subdivision of a tribal area.

In the western and northern parts of the country the village may consist of no more than a small scatter of dwellings, possibly without any public building or even a shop. In the Midlands, East Anglia and the south-eastern counties of England it can be a large settlement with all the facilities of a small market town and may sometimes contain several churches. The point at which a village becomes a town is difficult to determine; since the Middle Ages 'town' has been a legal term conferred by a borough charter. The granting of such charters was, however, haphazard – often ambitious lords were able to secure charters for small communities in the hope that the privileged trading conditions that resulted would promote the development of an urban settlement. While in some cases the settlement was successful in becoming a market centre, in others the settlement stagnated or even declined. Nevertheless, many such failed towns or 'rotten boroughs' as they were sometimes known were able to maintain their urban privileges, which often included parliamentary representation, into the nineteenth century. On the other hand many communities such as Ludlow (Salop) which were clearly towns, with defensive walls and other urban characteristics, were not legally defined as towns until the late Middle Ages. Thus in antiquity the legal definition cannot be used to distinguish towns from villages.

Other criteria, such as the possession of defences or public buildings, do not necessarily provide an adequate definition of town status, although from the late Saxon period onwards corporate defences are rarely found around villages. We therefore have to seek other methods of distinguishing a town. Today geographers would say that if the inhabitants of a settlement believe it to be a town then it is a town! There is a simple principle that may be applied, this being that if a settlement provides a range of services, administrative as well as economic, contains specialists and craftsmen and is dependent upon agricultural surplus from elsewhere, then it can normally be regarded as urban in character. Some of these functions may of course be carried out from villages, but the expression of these activities through the layout and buildings of a settlement are normally sufficient to distinguish town from village.

At the other end of the spectrum the problem is equally difficult. At what stage does a group of adjacent dwellings become a village? When is a particular farm unit considered to be isolated and at what stage does it form part of an interrelated cluster? The space between individual units will vary geographically and historically, but in general terms individual units can be said to belong to the same settlement if separated by less than 150 metres. Geographers facing the same problem of a distinction of a house unit (lieu habité) or a settlement unit (centre d'habitat) have also taken arbitrary separations ranging between 50 and 200 metres to distinguish dispersion from agglomeration. In the past historians have tended to evade the question except in very general terms and have taken the view that a place has defined itself as somewhere with a name.

We must, therefore, be content with a rule of thumb definition, that the inhabitants of a village will share certain communal features, such as access roads or water supply or a place of worship. Most village communities are, or have been, an expression of the need to organize some aspects of agricultural activity communally within a neighbourhood. The rights of the villagers within this territory amounted to an intricate mixture of claims, requiring constant cooperation between neighbours. The village endowed rights, obligations and ties upon its inhabitants. For the purpose of this book 'village' will also cover those nucleated communities which are generally believed to be of a lower order, and are often dependent upon larger villages. These include, hamlets, vills and townships which vary considerably in size and function in different parts of the country.

What are the sources available to the historian examining extant and past villages? Much of the evidence relating to our earliest villages is sparse and ambiguous in character, and we have to rely on the archaeological record far more than in the later period. Archaeology will provide us with house plans and tell us about the dwellings in which they lived: of what material the houses were built, how they were divided and how long they normally survived. The pottery and other artefacts recovered during excavation will indicate standards of living, the type of economy and the patterns of trading. The animal bones tell us about the types and standard of animals kept by the villagers, which cuts of meat they were eating and even something of their butchering techniques. Normally only items of pottery, bone and stone will survive, but in exceptional circumstances items made of skin, leather and wood will also have been preserved. Evidence in the form of pollen and insect remains can also be recovered from water-logged deposits and these tell us about the types of crops which were being cultivated, about the local environment and the changes in that environment. Essentially the archaeological record is a silent one, telling us what was there, but not why. As we move nearer to the present day there is, naturally enough, more surviving evidence, and indeed from the Middle Ages onwards we frequently have documentary records in addition to the standing buildings and vestiges of the original village plan to study.

One of the first things we must recognize is the problem of comparing evidence due to its differential survival. Our understanding both of individual sites and of the overall settlement pattern deteriorates as we move backwards in time. We can confidently describe the geography of rural England in the late nineteenth century on the basis of accurate documentary and cartographic evidence as well as the standing buildings and even photographic evidence. We would also be able to reconstruct reliably the manner in which the inhabitants earned their living, their social organization and their religious beliefs. If we move back five centuries to the late Middle Ages we could outline the general pattern and some of the detail, but we could be far less confident about the physical appearance of many settlements.

Were we to move back a further five hundred years to the ninth century there are very few aspects of village life which we could reconstruct with any degree of confidence, because of the particularly poor documentary and archaeological record of the mid Saxon period. In contrast if we were to move back a further half millennium we would be presented with a wide range of evidence of late Romano-British rural settlement. Our ability to interpret this evidence may be limited but it is available.

If we were to jump back yet a further thousand years to the sixth century BC, we would be totally reliant on fragmentary archaeological evidence which would provide us with the haziest of pictures of all aspects of rural life. For early Iron Age villages we are very fortunate if we have a plan of one or two dwellings with their outbuildings and paddocks. Our understanding of the social and economic complexion of the early communities will depend largely upon inference and analogy with contemporary societies operating at a similar stage of technological and economic development.

2 Village form and fabric

Any analysis of rural settlement is fraught with difficulties. The examination of human habitation past or present requires a multi-disciplinary approach, which by its very nature lends itself to mistakes and unjustified assumptions. The myths and mystical legends associated with the origins of many rural settlements are almost as acceptable as the antiseptic socio-economic explanations that have replaced them. Nevertheless we must persevere in order to try and understand more fully what we see. The layout of a settlement together with its buildings can tell us much of the evolution of that community.

Let us start with the site of the village; we should beware of jumping to conclusions. A great deal of argument has been generated in the past about geographical determinism and it should be emphasized that there is no inevitability about the distribution of settlement. The site may have been chosen for reasons which are not clear to us today, or the original reason may be masked by later developments. Indeed in most cases it is probably misleading to think of a village site being consciously chosen at all. The first occupant of a site may have been simply looking for a place to house only his family: subsequently a village may have developed on the spot because it occupied a convenient central position for surrounding traders. It is clear that many settlements began as groups of individual farms without any obvious pattern and the concept of the village is one which may have evolved over several generations. Rural settlements have shrunk, shifted or amalgamated, often making it difficult to identify the original site or sites, quite apart from defining an original choice of situation.

25

Villages in the landscape

There will, however, be quite obvious reasons for the choice of some sites: the availability of water, a river crossing, a road junction where advantage could be taken of passing traders or on the edge of woodland. Some villages occupy a knoll of dry land in an otherwise marshy area or lie along the flat bottom of a narrow steep-sided valley. But even in cases where there appears to be an obviously suitable site, other factors may have been responsible for the actual site on which the settlement developed.

It is not possible to examine a village in isolation from its surrounding fields, woods, commons and streams. Thus we should always be aware that we are examining only a detail of a much larger matrix, and that we cannot hope to understand a settlement without relating it to its economic hinterland. In the past geographers have tried to explain differences in settlement form and pattern because of ethnic or cultural variation, but today there is a tendency to argue that there are basic laws of settlement distribution which reflect the interaction of certain forces. The central place theory argues that given a fairly uniform physical base villages will be spaced at regular intervals in order to maximize the use of natural resources such as water, arable land, grazing land and woodland. Each community will lie at the most convenient site within the territory, in which all of these resources are available, in order to make the most effective use of them. Each resource will have a different value to the community and it therefore follows that those resources with the highest value, such as a source of water, will have a greater impact on the actual site which succeeds (Fig. 1). One of the most commonly quoted models is that of the springline village, sited along the bottom of a chalk escarpment on a water source. These are frequently regularly spaced and their territories (parishes) stretch in an elongated rectangular form from the bottom of the vale to the crest of the ridge. This provides each settlement with an equitable share of meadow, arable, rough grazing and woodland (Fig. 2).

This form of analysis can provide a useful starting point, but should not be pursued too relentlessly, since there are numerous factors involved, some of them incapable of being quan-

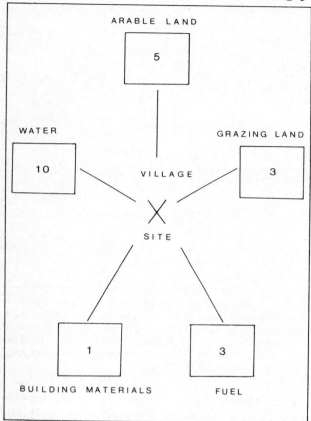

1. Village location. This diagram shows five basic elements in a primitive village economy. The figures assigned to each element represent a notional weighting which reflects the relative importance of each in the siting of a settlement. Thus according to this model it is far more important to be close to a source of water than a source of building material. The figures are hypothetical and will vary in space and time (after Chisholm 1968).

tified. Local political and economic forces may modify or even completely distort the simple pattern of the model. Some aspects of rural settlement lend themselves readily to quantitative analysis, particularly at periods of relative stability when factors such as mobility and resources are easily measured, for

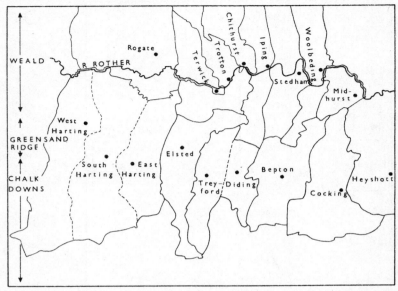

2.   Linear parishes along the South Downs of Sussex. Two locations are favoured for village siting, the spring line sites at the foot of the chalk escarpment and crossing points on the River Rother. The original pattern of regular rectangular parish boundaries has clearly been disturbed by their subdivision to accommodate later parish units based on the settlements lying to the south of the river (after Cunliffe 1973).

instance during the Middle Ages. However, with the increase of imponderable factors because of a broader area of choice and the intrusion of external factors systematic analysis becomes more difficult.

Then we have the fabric of the village itself, its buildings, plots and roads. We are not concerned here with cataloguing house-forms, building materials or architectural styles, although evidence from these sources must be taken into account. With the exception of the parish church, most of the buildings we see in villages date from after the 'Great Rebuilding' of rural England, which occurred around 1600. Despite the extensive and often uncritical use of synthetic and imported building material during the past hundred and fifty years, villages still reflect fairly faithfully the character of their underlying geology – the limestone villages of the Cotswolds, the timber and brick of the Midland claylands and the cob and thatch of Devon. The nature of the buildings will also tell us much about the history of the settlement – the church, chapel, school, almshouses, inn, alehouses, barns, industrial buildings, lock-up, dovecot and pound all have a story to relate.

The village plan

No generalization can satisfactorily explain the shapes of the thousands of villages in this country, and although one can point out common characteristics each settlement is unique and therefore must be examined individually in order to understand its present layout. It is important to realize, however, that almost all village shapes are capable of interpretation after careful analysis. We should be conscious of the physical form of the village: the relation between the houses and outbuildings, between the houses themselves, the road pattern and the internal and external boundaries of the settlement. The existence of working farms in the settlement and the way in which the land in the village was divided between its inhabitants should also be taken into account.

In the past, unless there were very obvious planned elements in a rural community, it was assumed that it had grown naturally. This is clearly not true; every village shape we see today is the product of a decision or series of decisions. Just as an old building is likely to have been renovated, added to and reshaped over a long period of time, so too have villages changed. These changes have not been limited to individual buildings, but have affected the whole form of the village. Similarly, it is difficult to overestimate the amount of settlement migration over much of Britain. Everywhere about us there are signs of a protracted process of movement. Our concept of a fixed village must surely be the result simply of our personal observations of settlement patterns over a decade or more. Even so, the rapidity of change that has occurred since the last war should tell us that rarely, if ever, is a settlement completely static.

In many cases it is possible to analyse the shape of a village

29

and break it down into its constituent elements. Villages change in time and place and the forces which led to their creation and development manifest themselves in a variety of ways. It is therefore not possible to generalize about the date at which villages assumed their present shape. For instance a planned regular medieval village may have decayed and appear today as a straggling uncoordinated settlement, while a village which was irregular in the Middle Ages can appear extremely regular if it was landscaped and remoulded as an estate village in the eighteenth or nineteenth century. In the case of Barnwell (Northants) the present village consists of two separate settlements which have now merged, and the two churches of All Saints and St Andrew are still both standing. At Durweston and Knighton (Dorset), the two villages grew together in the late Middle Ages and by 1580 their respective open-field systems were amalgamated and Durweston church dismantled. Another Dorset village, Alton Pancras, sits at the head of the River Piddle, and while the extended modern village is scattered over one kilometre it appears originally to have been two discreet settlements – Barcombe and Alton, each with its own open-field system. At Coombe Keynes (Dorset) the earthworks of a deserted settlement lie to the east and north-east of the parish church while the modern village lies on an entirely different east-west axis.

The shape of the village we see today will to a large extent be a reflection of the forces which have gone to make up that village. Thus the last period of regulation may dominate the village in the form of a green or square, or a uniform house style, or reflect the relative decay or phases of decay which may be seen in open areas as house platforms and earthworks. It should be appreciated that the village we see today is likely to consist of more than one unit: for example the church is likely to occupy the most ancient site, perhaps dating from before the Norman Conquest, adjacent to this may be an area which was regulated in the Middle Ages, and beyond an eighteenth- or nineteenth-century development next to a railway junction or canal. Opportunities for village development are not always present. Land ownership or tenure will normally dictate the availability of areas for village expansion

30

and it is likely to be the large estate, normally controlled by the lord of the manor, which has the most opportunity either to restrict or expand the village.

A useful distinction has been made between 'open villages' where there has been little development control and 'closed villages' where development has been carefully monitored by a dominant authority. This would originally have been the manorial lord but in recent years the role has to some extent been taken over by local government. It should not be assumed that a village has always been open or closed, or that it will remain so in perpetuity. Furthermore sections of a village may be closed while the remainder is open. It is true that properties will fall vacant from time to time to allow piecemeal development, but overall the shape of many of our villages appears to have been dictated or at least moulded by seigneurial control at some time in the past. Evidence of a large house, a park or monuments in the church will indicate the former presence of such a dominant authority.

Medieval villages operating open-field agricultural systems were in some senses closed. Tenant farmers had to operate within a fairly rigid framework of controls enforced by the lord through the manor court. Opportunities for change would therefore have been strictly limited; however, the evidence from excavations on deserted medieval sites would suggest that from time to time there were considerable changes both of individual buildings and sometimes of the village as a whole. One reason for the adoption of the 'closed' village principle by the post-medieval squire was that it limited the liability of a particular community to its poor. In the eighteenth and nineteenth centuries in particular it was chiefly used as a mechanism to restrict the number of labourers and thus keep the poor rates low.

Not only was there a marked difference in the layout of open and closed communities, but the character of the settlement varied greatly as well. The proprietor of a closed village was likely to regulate building strictly and oppose nonconformity, whereas nonconformist chapels were common in open communities. Similarly a puritanical proprietor often closed or prohibited the establishment of a public house. In contrast open townships were large, badly built, rambling villages crowded with small farmers, shopkeepers, artisans and land labourers. In the eastern counties open villages furnished the earliest gangs employed by large farmers for stone picking, potato setting, singling and lifting turnips, hay making and harvesting. Following enclosure the closed villages were particularly prone to depopulation.

The contrasting character of 'open' and 'closed' villages is well illustrated by Boynton and Burton Fleming (N. Yorks). The lord of Boynton, Sir George Strickland, owned all but eight acres of the whole parish at the time of enclosure in 1783. The neat uniform village has never had a nonconformist chapel or public house. The population remained at about 100 throughout the eighteenth and nineteenth centuries and labourers had to be brought in from outside. Although Strickland also held land in Burton Fleming there were other considerable proprietorial interests. This was a large 'open' village with a population rising from 240 in 1801 to 574 in 1851. There were numerous dissenters and by the mid nineteenth century there were three Methodist chapels as well as two public houses. The day of the closed village in the hands of one owner has not entirely passed, the notorious examples of Great Barrington (Glos) and Great Tew (Oxon) have demonstrated that a singleminded or neglectful landowner can still cause both the community and the village fabric to die.

If we look at the functions of the plan we will see that the village consists of two basic elements; common lands where all members of the community have rights of passage, grazing and gathering, and private land and buildings in which rights are restricted to individuals. Most of the common land consists of the routeways necessary for the movement of people and animals both within the settlement and leading from it to its associated fields, pastures and meadows. The thoroughfares include the village street onto which the majority of the dwellings normally face, the back lane which runs behind the house plots and often separates these from the fields, and particularly in the north of England, the cattle drift. This characteristically takes the form of a funnel-shaped track widening away from the village and gives direct access to an

I Upper Slaughter, Gloucestershire. Typical Cotswold village based on the framework of an open square, partly infilled lying in front of the church. The manor house (bottom right) effectively closes this part of the settlement.

II Braunston, Northamptonshire. An aerial view looking eastwards of a linear village occupying a ridge overlooking the Grand Union Canal (bottom right). The church, rectory, manor house and mill are grouped together at the western end. The tenement plots on the northern side extend to a back lane, in the fashion of medieval towns. The absence of a back lane and the irregular nature of the tenement plots on the south suggests to some observers that originally only the northern side was occupied.

III Nun Monkton, Yorkshire. A regulated village based on a triangular green. The church sits at the top of the green, possibly on a more ancient site.

IV Milburn, Cumbria. A highly regulated green village.

V   Castle Pulverbatch, Shropshire. A castle village of the twelfth century –
Church Pulverbatch, the original village in the parish lies two kilometres to
the south.

VI   An aerial view of Blanchland, Co. Durham. A model village built from
the ruins of the abbey by the earls of Creve in the mid eighteenth century to
house workers from the nearby lead mines.

area of common grazing. The passage of animals, carts and men often combined to lower the ground surface of the back lane until it was up to a metre below the crofts. If the ploughed field lands came right up to the village boundary, this would accentuate the contrast in height between the crofts and the field lands. The perimeter earthwork thus created was often used to prevent wild animals entering the village and domestic animals entering the fields.

The village green may be regarded as a spacious routeway which, because it lay at the heart of the settlement, was in the past used not only for common rights but also as a site of communal structures such as the smithy, pinfold, bakehouse, stocks and the village pond. In some cases it is difficult to distinguish between a broad linear street village and a narrow village green. Indeed in such examples as Heighington (Co. Durham) (Fig. 3) and Marsh Baldon (Oxon) it is tempting to believe that the very large greens represent a substantial part of the common grazing land. In the latter case, where the green is over half a hectare in size, we appear to be dealing with a marshland colonization settlement, set slightly apart from an earlier community based on the village church; there would probably not have been much common land in the marshy ground outside the plantation (Fig. 4).

Privately held land comprises a number of separate tenements, each of which normally contains at least one dwelling and an ancillary building. The churchyard with the church and the demesne with the manor house may be regarded as special types of such units present in some, but not all, villages (Plate I). In the north the individual plot was known as a toft or garth, although in subsequent legal usage the term was restricted to the house site while other associated enclosed plots were called crofts.

It is generally accepted that there are three principal categories of village plan: street or linear plans with ribbons or rows of house plots strung out along one or both sides of the street or long narrow green; green plans where the tenement compartments and roads are located around the margins of an open green of a variety of shapes; and agglomerated plans where toft compartments line more than one street with the

33

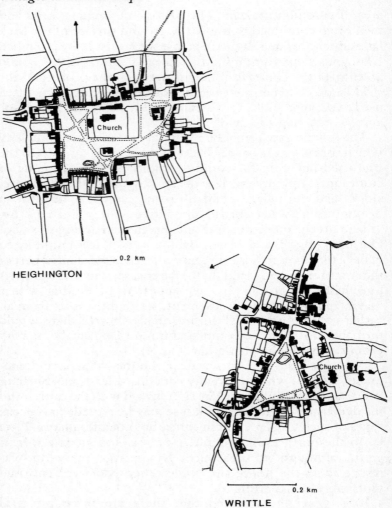

HEIGHINGTON

WRITTLE

3. *Top*. Heighington, County Durham. A classic example of a green village based on a large central open rectangle containing the church. In the south-east there has been some encroachment. *Bottom*. Writtle, Essex, a composite village plan, with a dominant triangular green unit as well as a secondary linear street unit at the east end. The siting of the church would suggest that both these elements were subsequent to a more ancient village plan.

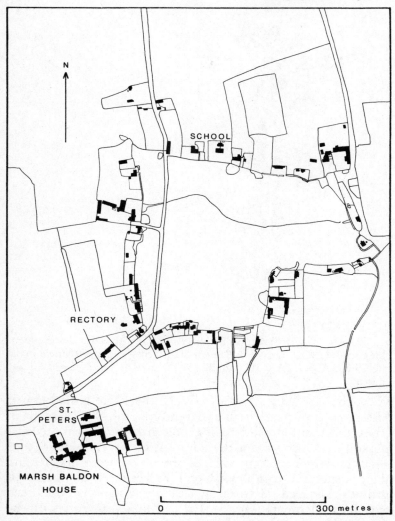

N

SCHOOL

RECTORY

ST.
PETERS

MARSH BALDON
HOUSE

0   300 metres

4. Marsh Baldon, Oxfordshire. The main village is based on a large square
green used as a common – the entry points to the common were gated until
recently. There has been extensive encroachment in the south-eastern
corner. The siting of the church and manor house indicates that the main
village plan is a secondary creation, perhaps dating from the early Middle
Ages.

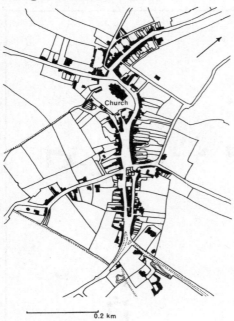

THAXTED

5. Thaxted, Essex. A composite village plan – with linear development along roads leading into the settlement. The success of the settlement in the late Middle Ages is attested by infilling in the market areas to the east of the church.

village houses lying at angles to each other. The agglomerated village is comprised of an apparently formless settlement of lanes, tenement plots, dwellings, often with no clear nucleus, possibly resulting from the addition of later buildings to a small settlement. Many villages are of course composite and their structural complexity will reflect various phases of growth. Thaxted in Essex is such a case, containing both green and linear elements (Fig. 5). Each of these categories can be further divided into regular or irregular forms and each type can be found either by itself or as a component of a complex. Regular forms may be defined as those where clear rows of tofts are present or where some standard shape of toft is repeated, such as a crescent or rectangular-shaped enclosure around a circular green.

36

Linear or street villages

Ostensibly these represent the most common form of village with dwellings and their enclosures laid out along the length of a street or road. Sometimes the street will broaden at the centre of the settlement in order to accommodate a market. In some cases such settlements extend over several kilometres. Appleton le Moors (N. Yorks) is a classic street village of the strictest regularity. The most common arrangement is where the dwellings face onto the road with the garden tenement plots extending at right angles to the road and parallel to each other.

The existence of such villages was often prompted by a geographical feature. For instance a street village might develop along a river bank where there was little room for lateral expansion, up a narrow valley, on one side of a stream, along the edge of marshland area or along a narrow hog's back of high ground where space is limited. They can, however, represent purely fortuitous developments along a road, and there may have been no geographical considerations in the make-up of their physical form. Indeed linear villages are common in East Anglia, where relief forms no barrier to settlement development as opposed to the west and south-west of Britain, where level land is only to be found in valley bottoms. For example, in north-west Cambridgeshire there are a number of settlements where dykes and water courses provide 'direction' to the form of settlement and a series of linear settlements strung out along main streets with little development along back lanes can be found. In some communities additional transport facilities may have been provided in the past by waterways running parallel to the main street in the position normally occupied by a back lane (Fig. 6) (Plate II).

The strictly orthodox linear village is not as common in Britain as it is in parts of north-west Europe where in some areas the majority of communities are in the form of street settlements. The complex local history of many areas and intensive use of land has meant that there will normally be some modification to this form, perhaps with the extension of a settlement along an adjoining road, or with the interference of a park or the construction of buildings along the back lane.

This has given rise to the development of multiple row settlements.

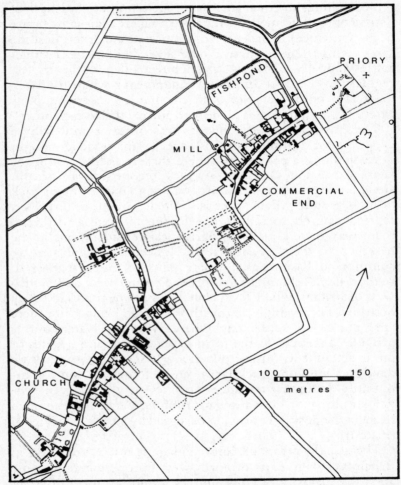

6. Swaffham Bulbeck, Cambridgeshire. The plan shows shrinkage at the centre of the old village and close to the church and the development of a virtually separate settlement outside the site of the gates of the former priory. This is called Commercial End, and formed the greater part of the hamlet of Newnham, which was a small canal port, dating from the seventeenth and eighteenth centuries (after R.C.H.M.).

38

The reasons for the creation of a linear village can be complex. At Skipwith (N. Yorks), the ancient settlement centre appears to have lain around the church of St Helens, the tower of which contains Saxon architecture. About the church are the earthworks of a former village and to the immediate south of the church there is a moated village site. The present village runs in a line between the church and a road running north-south which leads to York. About half the road is taken up by the rectory and a manor house, the latter presumably being a descendant of the moated site. The present Skipwith Hall is early Georgian with limited landscaping in the immediate vicinity. Its presence, however, has obviously prohibited further development at the western end of the village and now most of the houses are extended along the road on the eastern side of the hall leading to a small green with a pond at the road junction. Here there is an early eighteenth-century school, a primitive Methodist chapel, and two inns, one of which is called the Drover's Arms and has stables at the rear (Fig. 7). Close by there is a much decayed settlement at Aughton; here the church occupies a prominent site overlooking the broad flood-plain of the River Derwent. The village stretches back along a road towards Aughton Common. Next to the church are the earthworks of a motte and bailey castle and a large moated site now occupied by the rectory. In the village itself there are a number of small working farms. The adjacent village of Ellerton occupies a similar site, with the earthworks of a former priory around the church. A triangular green has developed at the east end of the village around a large pond – a common feature of such low lying villages.

In some cases it is difficult to distinguish between a failed town plantation, of which the single street element was intended to be the core, and a regular linear village. Henley in Arden (Warwicks), for example, is really no more than a village strung out along an axial road, although originally it was a medieval borough. Ruyton-XI-Towns (Salop) is a failed town which today appears as a village with two linear elements. The main street runs westwards from the church and castle site and has a number of empty tenement plots along it. The back lanes can be clearly identified together with a secondary element, which shows traces of decayed tenement boundaries in addition to the remnants of a back lane.

Some linear settlements are extremely long. Burwell (Cambs), for example, is three kilometres in length; the original nucleus lay at the southern end of the present village around St Mary's church. Other linear settlements represent the amalgamation of a number of communities. Cheselbourne (Dorset) is scattered for over one-and-a-half kilometres along

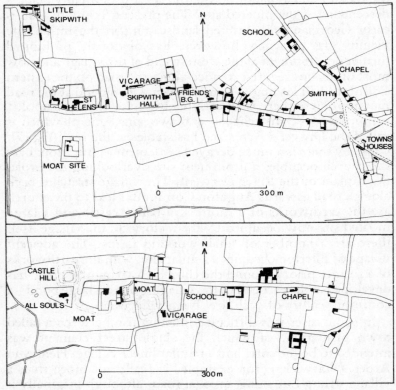

7. Skipwith (*top*) and Aughton. Adjacent linear settlements in a low lying area of North Yorkshire. Both have developed eastwards from an original nucleus around a church and manor site towards a line of north-south communication. Although both were relatively small communities in the late nineteenth century they contained a wide range of services. The plan of Aughton includes a large area of medieval earthworks.

the length of road that runs parallel to the stream after which it is named. The earthwork remains of former dwellings and closes are to be found among the existing cottages and open land to the south of St Martin's church. Some linear settlements are even more severely decayed, like Peswhere in Dorset, where earthworks occur intermittently over a length of seven kilometres from Winterbourne Houghton in the north to Winterbourne Whitechurch in the south. In the Middle Ages, there were seven minor separate settlements, now there are three villages and a scatter of farmsteads. An interesting variation to the linear theme is to be found at Hampton-on-Severn (Glos) where an extended village is made up of a number of component units all restricted to a narrow band of land along the bank of the river.

The place-name element 'long' is often to be found in the names of linear villages, for instance, Long Melford (Suffolk) which can boast both a Romano-British and a medieval street settlement (Fig. 8). The date at which such settlements acquired their prefix is of interest in the analysis of village forms, for instance, in the case of Longstow (Cambs), there is a much-decayed linear settlement, where the first use of the epithet 'long' can be traced back to 1268. In other cases the 'long' is added to distinguish settlements with identical names.

Green villages

Villages with a central open space are common throughout Britain. For instance, it has been estimated that almost half of the settlements in the former County Durham include a green or green-like element. The green can be circular, square, rectangular or an indefinite shape. In most cases the dwellings will face onto the central open area. In many settlements, however, the green is an independent unit and there are other elements to the village. For instance Finchingfield (Essex) has one small triangular green to the east of the church, a linear row to the north of the church and a large hourglass-shaped green to the west. Stanford in the Vale (Oxon) has two greens called Church Green and Upper Green. In some cases the green may be a secondary and barely noticeable element. In

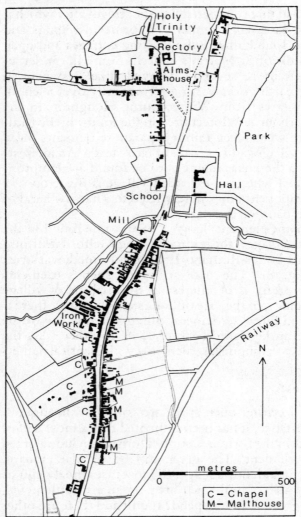

8.   Long Melford, Suffolk. A small fossilized town made up of two basic
elements – a triangular green and a linear unit, interrupted by the siting of
Melford Hall. The cloth industry ceased to be of any real importance by the
seventeenth century and although a modest attempt at industrial development was later attempted the number of malthouses depicted on this late
nineteenth-century map demonstrates the agrarian base of the settlement.

the case of Abthorpe (Northants) a tight rectangular village green containing the church now forms only a minor element in an extended village plan.

We can no longer regard the village green as an integral part of Anglo-Saxon settlement. The village greens we see today have developed or were created over a considerable period from the late Saxon period onwards, and evidence of 'greens' even appears in the earthworks of prehistoric and Romano-British earthwork sites. The origins of greens are far from clear and there is no single explanation. Some were formed at the time a regulated village was created. Some may have arisen out of the widening of two intersecting roads to allow for a variety of routes, for instance, Comberton (Cambs). Others may have originated as market places and fairgrounds; it is possible that the fashion for these between the twelfth and fourteenth centuries, when licences and charters were obtained by hundreds of manors, led to the creation of open spaces within the village. Some settlements appear to have been altered radically in order to accommodate markets. For instance, at South Cave (N. Humberside) there is a completely separate green element called Market Street. In some cases it is probable that small village greens represent market areas sited in front of the parish church; a good example of this is to be seen at Chittlehampton (Devon) (Plate XVIII).

The example of East Witton (N. Yorks) is also an interesting one. The original settlement lay around the ancient church of St Ella. In the late thirteenth century the hamlet came into the hands of the monks of nearby Jervaulx Abbey who apparently developed a new village around a green, probably for the market and fair for which they acquired rights in 1307. The highly regulated plan which appears on an early seventeenth-century map almost certainly provides us with a clear case of village planning from around 1300 (Fig. 9). The plan also indicates that the new settlement may have been regulated by the process known as sun division which is discussed on p. 47.

It has been suggested that in East Anglia, where green villages were the most common form of rural settlement, the greens were frequently sited in the wetter parts of the parish, either in damp valleys or on poorly drained boulder clay

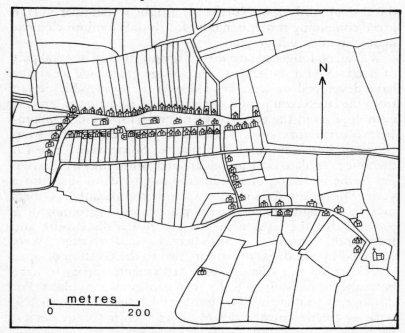

N

metres
0   200

9.   East Witton, North Yorkshire. A plan of 1627 shows that the original village nucleus lay to the south-east of the village which appears to have been replanned by the monks of nearby Jervaulx Abbey in the early fourteenth century. The village plan conforms to the arrangement by sun division or *solskifte*.

plateau soils. It is probable that because these areas were not initially attractive for cultivation they had been used for common grazing before the Norman Conquest. As pressure on land resources grew in the early Middle Ages they often became focal points for new enlarged planned settlements. The ancient common would have been attractive for the site of the new village, because it would have released the land on which the old village stood and would also have enabled a fairly spacious redesign of the settlement (see Fig. 18). A particularly interesting example of green creation was at Reach (Cambs) where a length of Devil's Dyke was destroyed to create a rectangular green at a secondary stage in the

44

development of the village plan. Thus the green village along with other forms of regulated rural communities in the early Middle Ages appears to have developed as a response to population pressure.

Some greens in the north also appear to have been associated with defence, the green being used as a refuge to which animals were herded in time of attack. The narrow entrances were such that they could be closed and defended easily. This characteristic is well illustrated at Milburn (Cumbria), where a regulated compact community lies around a rectangular green. It also seems to have been associated both then and in earlier times with colonization, notably of woodland. In Dorset some of the early hamlets are associated with commons and greens; these are often roughly triangular in shape, and appear to represent land left for pasture when the surrounding territory was enclosed from the waste into small irregular fields. At Hawkridge (Somerset) which lies at about 300 metres above sea level, in the area of the former Forest of Exmoor, there is a cluster of dwellings around a small green which lies before the Norman church of St Giles. It is possible that this green settlement, like many others in the area, grew up around a forest chapel. It has been suggested that the double green plan may be particularly common in areas of heavy woodland. Syresham (Northants) for example, which lies on the edge of Whittlewood Forest has such a plan, with one loop associated with the church and another a few hundred yards to the south, both greens having been heavily encroached upon.

In some cases the green will have been partially or completely enclosed. At Heighington (Co. Durham) there has been considerable encroachment in the south-western corner apart from one or two other blocks of buildings which have been built. The shape of the green is not so apparent on the ground because of the central position of the church and the encroachments. In the plan (see Fig. 3) it can be seen that a complete outer ring-road has developed on the back lanes, except in the areas where infringement has taken place, and it should be noted that because of the basic layout of the settlement even encroachments can have a planned regular appearance.

The corners of the green represent the most natural entry points, and most of the roads entering the central part of a village are narrow and have a tortuous approach. We often find that in the case of a triangular green such as that at Writtle (Essex) there are two main routeway entrances at the eastern and northern corners, while there is a small cul-de-sac in the western corner (see Fig. 3). In this case a small subsidiary unit has developed in the form of an elongated square beyond the eastern angle of the green. We find that some estate villages, such as Coneysthorpe which lies outside Castle Howard Park (N. Yorks) consist of a wide rectangular cul-de-sac sited in a shallow valley at right angles to the approach road. The position of the church, in this case in one of the blocks of the green, suggests that it was contemporary with the creation of the settlement.

In a large number of cases we find that the green has been sacrificed and built over; for instance at Marham la Fen (Lincs) it has been completely encroached upon. Many greens survived until the period of Parliamentary Enclosure, when they were enclosed along with other areas of common land in the parish. In the case of Munslow (Salop) the green had probably originated when the village became the centre of a hundred in the early Middle Ages, but it was extinguished by an Act of Parliament in 1838 when it was auctioned for £60 to pay for the costs of enclosure.

In some cases the presence of a central open space may represent a failed town plantation, for example, Montgomery (Powys), ostensibly still a town, has an impressive market square overlooked by a town hall, but its size and functions can be compared to many Midland villages. Villages with large market squares can also be found in western England, where there is a rather dispersed settlement pattern; here the large village performs the function of a market town. A group of these communities are to be found in Herefordshire; Weobley, for instance, has a large market square to the north of a very large parish church, and to the north again lie the earthwork remains of a castle.

Just one note of warning. Not all open spaces in the centre of villages are greens, although they might appear to be common

46

to the community as a whole. In some cases a dominant authority has developed a large garden or small park in the heart of the community, often with the result that roads are diverted and access prohibited. Often in plans such areas will have the appearance of an open green.

Planned villages

It is now generally accepted that many villages, like towns, were deliberately laid out and that the plans of such villages with their regular streets and tenement boundaries tell of the origins of such communities. Plantations of recent centuries have been recognized for some time: some were built on the edge of parks in association with a great house, others had their origin in land reclamation or settlement schemes, or in industrial development. All of them were built under the directing force of one man or group of men, and their plans were almost always direct and simple. The classic example of a plantation is Milton Abbas (Dorset), built in about 1786 to replace a small market town which lay too close to the manor house for the comfort of the first Viscount Milton (see Fig. 24).

What has only recently emerged, however, is that plantations of the eighteenth and nineteenth centuries continue a tradition of regulated settlement which extends back to the Middle Ages and earlier. The case of green villages has been discussed above, but there appears to have been a considerable amount of village redesign in the years 1100–1300. It has been suggested that the characteristic layout of medieval villages with regular parallel plots spaced around a green or street was a conscious act of planning known as *Solskifte* or 'sun division'. The main element of the process was that the village was laid out and tenement plot widths were proportionate to the assessment figures of the agricultural holdings attached to each farmstead. The plots were normally placed in two facing rows and were considered to be arranged in a clockwise direction around the village. This corresponded to the course of the sun around the sky – hence the term 'sun division'. The order of the plots was followed for the strips in the open fields, so that

47

everywhere a man's strips lay between those of his neighbours in the village (see Fig. 9). This is a highly ingenious concept that has been convincingly demonstrated to have operated in Scandinavia and a number of possible examples have also been identified in England, notably in the north-east.

Quite apart from the topographical evidence, excavation on the sites of deserted medieval villages has shown that many sites were laid out afresh from time to time. For instance, the village of Wawne (Humberside) was redesigned in the fourteenth century and at Wharram Percy (N. Yorks) three distinct planned phases of growth between the eleventh and fourteenth centuries have been identified. At Seacourt (Oxon) a regular north-south street of stone-built houses was added to the previously all-timber village in the thirteenth century.

There are some indications that the great spate of town plantation, with the creation of many newly laid out market towns in the twelfth and thirteenth centuries was mirrored in the countryside by the establishment of new or extended rural settlements. Some of these were created to absorb a rapidly growing population, and hopefully to attract trade, eventually leading to the development of a profitable commercial centre. In many cases, the process appears to have been one of imitation, and in areas where there are newly created towns it is useful to look at nearby villages to see if traces of medieval regulation can be identified.

In some northern villages the basic plan type appears to have originated before 1200 and traces of twelfth-century property boundaries can sometimes be identified (Plates III and IV). In some areas this regularity is a product of reorganization following the results of the devastation caused by the 'harrying of the north', by William I. Wheldrake in the Vale of York appears to be such an example. Thus many of the well-ordered villages of the north-east, originally believed to be a product of the Anglo-Saxon settlement, date from a considerably later period. The initial examination of some types of villages in the Welsh borderland also suggests that regular villages may have been laid out afresh after large-scale destruction in the post-Conquest period. This replanning was often associated with the creation of a small castle (Plate V). In the latter case defence

48

may have been a major factor in refashioning the village shape, as the tenement plots often occupy a road leading away from the castle entrance, or assume a horseshoe shape as if forming an outer bailey. In other cases, such as Corfe (Dorset), topographical limitations have regulated the shape of the settlement so that the horseshoe form of the village represents a response to the restrictions imposed by the Corfe valley and the desire to establish a broad market place for trading purposes, rather than any defensive considerations.

Indeed defensive features are rarely to be seen in village plans: the tradition of hillfort settlements appears largely to have died out during the late Anglo-Saxon period. Although some features of village topography such as greens may have sometimes played a defensive role after the Norman Conquest, the corporate defence of rural settlement seems to have lapsed. In contrast private defensive works such as the castle and moat are commonly found in the Middle Ages. Village plans may include relict features of early defensive structures, such as the alignment of Roman town walls (Fig. 10) or the fortifications of a Saxon *burh*. However, the belief that villages with place-names containing the element 'bury' (Old English *burg* – fort, town) were in some way defended has been disproved.

Regular medieval villages often appear to have been associated with castles, monasteries or the gatehouses of large country houses. Sometimes they were built in linear form along the road leading to the gateway, as at Portchester (Hants) and Kimbolton (Cambs) where additional development has occurred along the back lane (Fig. 11) or around a triangular square or rectangular green in front of the institution. At Blanchland (Co. Durham) the ancient village occupied a triangular green in front of the Augustinian Abbey; interestingly enough an eighteenth-century planned settlement was added to the village on the site of the abbey (Plate VI). In the case of Muchelney (Somerset) a small green village built in the style of the abbey buildings still survives to provide a picturesque backcloth to the ruins of the Benedictine Abbey. Because of their siting such villages have often been firmly regulated over a long period and therefore tend to maintain an

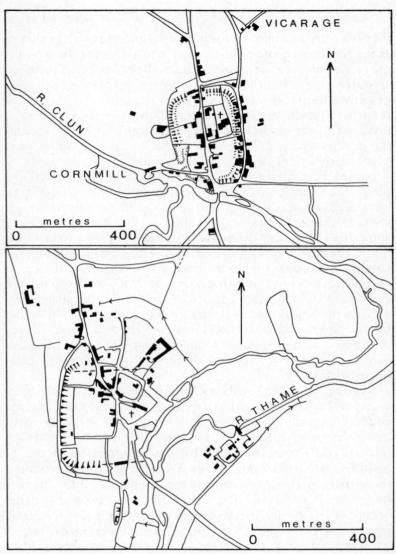

10.   Leintwardine, Hereford (*top*) and Dorchester on Thames, Oxford-shire, are both modern villages lying on the sites of small Romano-British towns. Traces of earthworks are visible in both cases: at Leintwardine the road pattern still retains elements of the Roman system, while at Dorchester the Roman plan has been superseded by one based on the Saxon and medieval abbey.

50

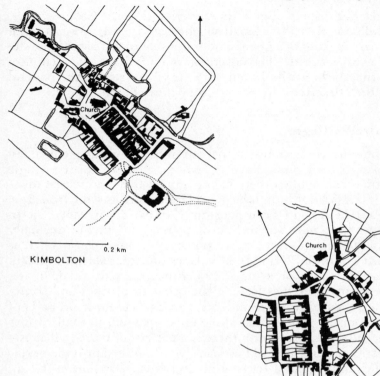

KIMBOLTON

SHERSTON

11. *Top*. Kimbolton, Cambridgeshire. The village appears to have been replanned in the early Middle Ages in relationship to the castle, which sits at the southern end of the settlement. The church may have already been in existence and incorporated into this plan or could have been contemporary with the redesign and assigned a segment of the new layout. *Bottom*. Sherston, Wiltshire. A good example of a small compact market town laid out in the thirteenth century alongside a small existing settlement. The plan preserves the typical form of a small planted borough based on a broad high street. In both settlements there has been secondary development along one of the back lanes.

51

'unspoilt' aspect. On a spur overlooking the Stour Valley, Chilham (Kent) is a small village based on a compact open square in front of a grand Tudor house which occupies the site of an earlier castle. The village sits outside the brick gatehouse, so that the house looks out onto the village square and beyond to the attractive fifteenth-century flint church.

Paired villages

It has already been noted that a number of villages which lay close to each other have grown together to form a single settlement, while others have retained their individual identities. It is a tradition which goes back at least to the Iron Age; Grantchester and Trumpington (Cambs), for instance, sit on either side of a stream. Such paired settlements normally straddle a boundary, either physical or administrative. It is quite common to find twin villages on either side of a stream sharing a ford or bridge. Sometimes the pair amalgamate, sometimes one dies leaving the other to prosper and sometimes they continue as independent discrete units. In parts of the country, for instance along the Cotswolds in Oxfordshire and Northamptonshire, there is a pattern of paired villages – Eastleach Turville and Eastleach Martin (Glos) provide a typical example, Little Barrington and Great Barrington (Glos), Sibford Gower and Sibford Ferris (Oxon). The origins of such settlements are often quite obvious in terms of physical geography, others in administrative terms, but some are less easy to interpret. Two manors in a medieval village may give rise to the appearance of split settlements, sometimes even resulting in two parish churches in one community. An instance of such local rivalry is to be seen at Swaffham Prior (Cambs) (Plate VII).

SELECT BIBLIOGRAPHY

Allison, K. J., *The East Riding of Yorkshire Landscape* (1976).
Baker, A. R. H. and Harley, J. B. (eds), *Man Made the Land* (1973).

Chisholm, M., *Rural Settlement and Land Use* (1962).

Finberg, J., *Exploring Villages* (1958).

Fowler, P. J. (ed.), *Recent work in Rural Archaeology* (1975).

Holderness, B. A., 'Open and Closed Parishes in England in the Eighteenth and Nineteenth Centuries', *Agricultural History Review*, xx (part ii).

Roberts, B. K., *Rural Settlement in Britain* (1977).

Sharp, T., *The Anatomy of the Village* (1946).

3   The earliest villages

Today one would only dare speculate on just how ancient the foundations of our oldest villages are. Some archaeologists consider that there are areas of preferred settlement: those places which because of aspect, soil conditions, availability of water or ease of communication are more likely to be occupied than others – an application of the central place theory to ancient occupation sites. A settlement may not, and almost certainly will not, remain static over many centuries, but will move around in various forms within the preferred area. Thus although there may not be continuous occupation of specific sites, there may well have been continuous occupation of a general location. Often the framework of the agrarian landscape will survive more effectively than the settlements themselves; holdings and estates may pass almost unaltered for centuries, sometimes through periods of fundamental cultural and ethnic change, while the dwellings and communities they serve will alter radically.

An example of this form of continuity is to be found at Garton (N. Yorks) where there is evidence of a Neolithic settlement which was subsequently followed by Bronze Age burials, an Iron Age settlement and cemetery, a Romano-British farmstead and Anglian cemeteries, both pagan and Christian. All of these sites lie within a kilometre of the modern village. Similarly at Aldwincle (Northants) archaeological evidence from the Neolithic to the early Saxon period has been found within a kilometre radius. At Lakenheath (Suffolk) recent fieldwork has identified a concentration of archaeological material dating from the late Neolithic to the Anglo-Saxon period within a kilometre of the parish church. In some instances it is even possible to distinguish earthwork sites which have continued in use over a considerable period. For instance at Park Brow near Cissbury in central Sussex limited excavations on an extensive earthwork site indicated in the 1920s that there was a village community on the site from the late Bronze Age into the Roman period (Fig. 12). Such traces obviously cannot be interpreted as continuous village settlement, but simply point to the possibility of consistent occupation and agricultural activity within a particular area. In recent years the number of places where this can be demonstrated has slowly increased, and future full-scale excavation of a large area could provide definitive evidence of a settlement surviving on or near the same site over several millennia.

Why has man found it necessary to live in village groups? The answers are complex and there is little general agreement about the optimum size of human grouping: this too will vary according to the level of technological ability. During the late Mesolithic period (middle Stone Age), man changed from being primarily a peripatetic food hunter and collector to being a settled farmer. The colonization of land for crop-growing and animal husbandry necessitated a more settled way of life, and in many cases the best way of organizing this was in communal groups, situated near a source of water. It was also easier to defend a nucleated settlement than a scatter of isolated farmsteads; in case of attack by man or beast the village animals could be rounded up and driven to safety inside an enclosure. The need to feed a growing population also induced nucleated rural communities and sowing, ploughing, reaping and threshing became communal activities. With limited land available the need to regulate farming activities became increasingly great, as indeed was the pressure to share in common certain resources, such as draught animals and ploughs.

Despite a growing body of evidence relating to the earliest settlers it is still difficult to talk of prehistoric villages in general terms. Much thinking about the form of early rural settlement has in the past been rather imprecise and a great deal of theory on this topic has now been discredited. The problem

55

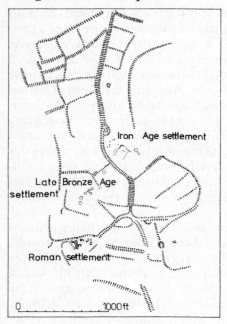

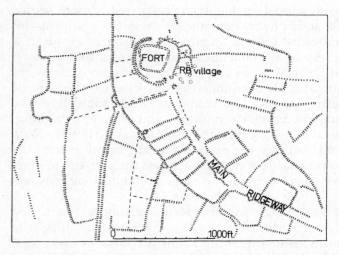

12. Parkbrow (*top*) and Thundersbarrow Hill (*bottom*). Prehistoric and Romano-British earthwork sites in Sussex (after Cunliffe 1973).

that is common to the whole of prehistory is the uneven nature of the surviving evidence, which makes it virtually impossible to think in terms of national, regional or even local patterns of settlement. The evidence from excavation has in the past been misleading. The old view that the settlement at Glastonbury 'Lake Village' (Somerset) was a community of some ninety close-set huts has been demonstrated to be untrue, based on the conflation of several phases of occupation into one; in reality the settlement seems to have had only twelve huts at its maximum extent. As a result of this archaeologists have been rather reluctant to make firm precise statements about the status of an individual settlement or about native settlement patterns in early prehistory.

Quite apart from doubts about the contemporaneity of structures within a site there are considerable problems associated with the interpretation of apparently contemporary buildings. The absence of documents to give us details of cultivation practices and inheritance customs means that the interpretation of often incomplete archaeological evidence must be highly speculative. In many instances it is not possible to be certain if an excavated settlement simply represents a single farmstead with subsidiary buildings or is in fact a hamlet of separate farming units. Similarly, even where it is possible to distinguish a group of contemporary farms we cannot be sure that this simply represents an extended family group.

Another factor to be taken into consideration when examining early rural settlement is the uneven survival of sites. Over much of southern and eastern Britain continuous agricultural activity has all but levelled or destroyed much of the evidence. Sites are identified by fieldwork, aerial photography or by accident (for it is in lowland Britain that most rescue archaeology is carried out in response to destructive agencies of one form or another). In the highland zone, on the other hand, many early sites survive in earthwork form, and although a considerable amount of field recording has been undertaken few settlements have been fully excavated.

Another problem common to all prehistoric and indeed protohistoric sites is our frequent failure to identify sites which are occupied for only a very short period or are occupied seasonally on the basis of field evidence alone – excavation is required to demonstrate seasonal differences in the artefacts. The practice of transhumance, that is the movement of animals sometimes over long distances for grazing purposes, appears to have been common in prehistoric Britain, and indeed survived in parts of the country until the eighteenth century. Herdsmen moving to upland or valley floodplain pasture (land not generally available for grazing during the winter) would construct temporary shelters often grouped along a droveway leading to the pasture. Such temporary communities are easily mistaken for permanent villages, although some shealings in northern Britain which started life as seasonal settlements were eventually occupied on a permanent basis. Some of the recently excavated cropmark sites on the Upper Thames river terraces in Oxfordshire have been identified as representing part of a transhumance pattern in the Bronze and Iron Age.

Settlement in the Neolithic and Bronze Age

It is generally accepted that the first substantial farming activity associated with permanent or semi-permanent settlement in Britain was at the beginning of the fifth millennium BC. These farmers were equipped with stone hoes, with which they tilled the light soils carrying a thin woodland cover. There are clear indications that in parts of the country they worked the heavier soil as well. We know tantalizingly little of their homesteads but the remains of their substantial ritual causewayed camps such as that at Windmill Hill (Wilts), are impressive. In the later Neolithic period and the early Bronze Age the causewayed camps were superseded by henge monuments and a variety of other large communal structures, which continued the tradition of ritual and trading centres. Some authorities argue that early patterns of settlement which later developed as multiple estates can be traced in the regions around these central points, but as yet this theory remains unproven.

It is clear from investigation in eastern Europe and the Near East that Neolithic communities often lived in quite substan-

58

tial nucleated villages. The evidence for Britain, however, is slight, and although we can be reasonably certain that there was a considerable population in the Neolithic period, we know little of the settlements in which people lived. However, in the far north of the country some Neolithic villages have been examined. In Orkney the village of Skara Brae and its companion Rinyo, together with the Shetland examples of Jarlshof and Stanydale have survived because of their robust stone construction and their isolated siting (Plate VIII). Although we cannot be sure of the economic and social organization of these sites we can be reasonably certain that they represent nucleated farming communities, at least during the later phases of occupation.

Likewise circular stone foundations of dwellings of this period have been found in Devon and Cornwall; elsewhere, however, only rare signs of Neolithic timber dwellings have occurred, and this is in marked contrast to the evidence from the continent where extensive work has been carried out on Neolithic timber houses arranged in villages. The evidence from Britain is tantalizingly slight. A timber structure measuring some 6 metres by 4.6 metres was found on Haldon Hill (Devon) and another about the same size at Clegyr Boia (Dyfed). In recent years work on other sites such as Barford (Warwicks), Highfleet (Derby) and Peterborough (Cambs) has provided further information concerning the native Neolithic dwellings. Nevertheless, the accumulated evidence is still insufficient for us to make any generalized statements about the pattern of rural settlement during the British Neolithic. There are grounds to believe, however, that quite apart from seasonal movement there was a considerable degree of mobility in the early settlements, implying that movement was necessary to fully exploit the agricultural potential of a region.

We can assume that as with all cultural changes there must have been a long period of overlap, so that as farmers were settling into communities, hunters and gatherers continued with their way of life, hunting being of importance as a source of food to the farming groups as well. As we move into the Bronze Age there is evidence that both activities were taking

59

place side by side. At Staple Howe, Knapton (N. Yorks) it is possible that the occupants of a nucleated settlement were growing grain and rearing animals on the Wolds and hunting and fishing on the lower ground of the Vale of Pickering at the same time.

The first metal users in Britain, the Beaker and Bronze Age people, were prolific builders; they constructed numerous round barrows and cairns, and traces of their activity in the form of pottery, weapons, tools and implements indicates that Bronze Age dwellings must have been numerous. So far, however, they have proved to be almost as elusive as those of the Neolithic period, except in Orkney, the Shetlands and parts of central Scotland.

In Wessex, despite the brilliance of the culture shown by the graves and other monuments, we have little real idea of how or where people lived. Recent excavations in Sussex, however, have provided us with some clues as to the nature of Bronze Age occupation. A nucleated settlement in which there are about six enclosures lying adjacent to each other, forming an elongated area some 140 by 15 metres has been found at Itford Hill (E. Sussex). Excavation has uncovered much of the site plan, suggesting differences in both size of house type and function, and implying perhaps social differences as well as specialized working areas. The main palisaded enclosure contained a single large living hut about seven metres in diameter together with three smaller ancillary huts. The three adjacent palisaded enclosures each contained one or two huts. Further west along a hollow approach road were two apparently unenclosed huts with a small banked enclosure between, possibly for cooking. Three isolated huts were excavated bringing the total to at least thirteen dwellings. This arrangement has been interpreted in terms of a central establishment for a patriarch around which a number of other family units have clustered, giving rise to a substantial hamlet. It is interesting to note that here too the site enjoyed a relatively short life, of perhaps no more than twenty-five years.

The granite moorlands of Devon and Cornwall are covered in prehistoric settlement sites of all periods. On Dartmoor the best-known sites have occurred in enclosures known as pounds, within which circular foundations of dwellings are often found. One of the best known examples of these is Grimspound (Devon) (Fig. 13). The site is contained within a massive perimeter wall which was largely reconstructed in the last century. It covers some 1.6 hectares and contains sixteen dwelling huts, six or seven store huts, and a few cattle pens. The huts vary in diameter from 2.4 to 4.6 metres. Each of the dwellings has a hearth and many contain traces of central posts to support the roof, whereas the store huts are much less substantial. Cattle pens were built against the pound wall and it is believed that its inhabitants must have been pastoralists, occupying the site from around 1000 to 800 BC. It is possible that small-scale cultivation was carried out within the enclosed area, and indeed at Riders Rings there are several small walled garden plots, although evidence of large-scale agricultural activity is absent. Some of these settlements show signs of development – at Legis Tor a sequence of walls can be traced demonstrating that the enclosed area was greatly increased in three successive stages but it is only possible to speculate if this was the result of population pressure, or the amalgamation of small hamlets into a larger nucleated community.

There is a second type of settlement in the south-west, that is the unenclosed village where clusters of circular huts are linked together by low stone walls, creating multi-angular enclosures which could well have served as both cultivation plots and paddocks for stock at different times of the year. Sometimes these villages reach considerable proportions, for instance no fewer than sixty-eight apparently associated huts have been identified at Standon Down, but not all sites are so strictly nucleated. At Bodrifty, for instance, about a dozen huts have been identified, linked together by stretches of walling, while at Roughton on Bodmin Moor, huts and their attached enclosures spread for about half a mile along a track. Here we may well be dealing with a linear development representing settlement shift over a considerable period of time.

Many of these settlements have traces of field systems attached to them, indicating some form of agricultural activity. At Standon Down, St Breward (Cornwall) the second phase of the village was associated with the system of long

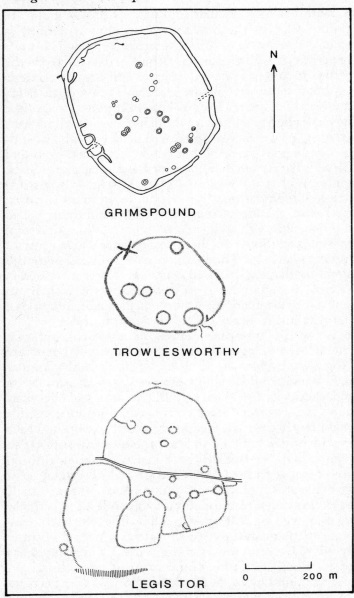

N

GRIMSPOUND

TROWLESWORTHY

LEGIS TOR

0   200 m

13.   Bronze Age pounds in south-western England.

narrow plots, or fields, separated by walls which were largely created as a result of surface stone clearance. However, many of the Dartmoor sites sit well above the present margin of cultivation. Standon Down, for instance, lies at over 450 metres above sea level reflecting the kind of climate of the Bronze Age period. There appears to have been climatic deterioration during the first millennium BC and this resulted in the abandonment of the Dartmoor sites. In west Cornwall, however, the elevation of the ground is considerably less than further east and this allowed occupation of the village sites to continue into the Iron Age and Roman periods.

Recently some earthwork sites away from the traditional chalk downland areas have been reinterpreted as likely to be of prehistoric date. The rectangular form of enclosure, so characteristic of Roman and later periods, has been demonstrated to be of middle Bronze Age date at Shearplace Hill in Dorset, where there also seems to have been a recognizable road system. Perhaps one of the best guides to the extent of early settled farming is the evidence of field and ranch boundaries. Recent work on sealed peat deposits in Ireland has uncovered Neolithic field boundaries and in Britain there is extensive evidence of the nature and extent of Bronze Age Celtic fields still surviving on the chalk uplands. Continuing analysis of the fields, their geography and their productive capacity should help us to understand more fully the nature of early farming communities.

Rural settlement in the Iron Age

The outstanding field monument of the Iron Age is the hillfort, there being something like 1500 sites in England and Wales alone, varying in size between one-tenth of a hectare to over 40 hectares (Fig. 14). They are found predominantly in Wales and the south-west but there is an uneven spread throughout the rest of the country, although they are largely absent from eastern England (Plate IX). One's initial reaction is to exclude this type of site from any discussion on villages, as until fairly recently they were thought to have been built and occupied for a relatively short period from about 300 BC to the time of the Roman Conquest. As such they would have been shortlived and abnormal features of rural settlement, their chief characteristic being their defensive features which are not associated with settlements of other periods. However, recent work has shown that not only do the hillforts have

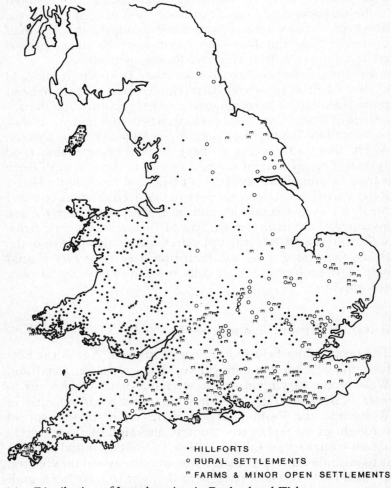

· HILLFORTS
○ RURAL SETTLEMENTS
ᵐ FARMS & MINOR OPEN SETTLEMENTS

14. Distribution of Iron Age sites in England and Wales.

a much longer history, starting in a simple form during the late Bronze Age, but that they were also in use during the Roman period, and many hilltop sites were reoccupied after the Romans left through to the Anglo-Saxon period. Cadbury Castle, in south-east Somerset, for example, was occupied in the Neolithic, Late Bronze and Early Iron Ages. Subsequently it was refortified in the post-Roman and late Saxon period. Thus the defended hilltop site can be shown to have had an extremely long history of use in Britain.

Added to this is the evidence that has come from recent excavations of the interior of some hillforts. Signs of permanent or seasonal occupation appear on the surface of the interior of many hillforts in the form of circular ditches, platforms or stone foundations. Most hillforts appear to have been lived in by communities of hamlet or village size – apparently the same fort was often successively occupied and reoccupied several times over the centuries. Recently, detailed surveys and excavations have begun to throw light on the layout of these settlements. There is good evidence that most forts were intended by their builders as sites for permanent occupation, although in some major forts the settlement seems always to have had the character of a defended village, not the stronghold or castle of a military caste. There is substantial evidence for wooden houses and other buildings, and in the highland zone cases of stone built huts and houses appear to have been common. Some upland sites were occupied seasonally only during the months of high ground grazing, but were occupied for much longer periods when there was danger of attack; this latter appears to have been the function of the hillfort of Tre'r Ceiri in North Wales. This fort contains about 150 huts which were in use during the Roman period, although occupation on site probably began during the Iron Age. Below the fort are a number of enclosed farmsteads of the same period; it has been argued that Tre'r Ceiri served as the summer abode and refuge for the lowland community. It has also been suggested that many hillforts formed the nuclei of multiple estates, and that many later conventional villages formed part of such estates in an earlier guise and were responsible for the construction and upkeep of the forts.

Villages in the landscape

The occupation of the interior was not normally continuous from the first building of the defence to the latest use of the site. It consisted instead of intermittent reoccupations; each reoccupation was probably intended to be permanent but reoccupations were sometimes separated from preceding and succeeding occupations by considerable gaps of time. As with later rural settlement sites there is evidence that some hillfort buildings were reconstructed several times during a single phase of habitation.

Excavation has rarely been extensive enough to find clear evidence for the total layout of a settlement within a fort. Nevertheless there are some indications that in some forts there was a random and disordered scattering of individual houses over a large part of the interior, and others where they seem to have had a population of moderate size living more densely packed together than people apparently did in settlements outside hillforts. On other sites, notably Maiden Castle (Dorset), Croft Ambrey (Hereford & Worcester), Danebury (Hants) and Crickley (Glos), there are hints of regulated community planning where houses and subsidiary buildings are arranged along roads, but as yet insufficient excavation has taken place to enable us to see if this is generally true.

What does appear to be true and is particularly pertinent to our discussion is that hillforts do not appear to have operated any exceptional form of economy. Although each hillfort may have had its own political territory, forts do not seem to have been centres of great economic power whose inhabitants dominated and impoverished all subject peasantry in the surrounding area as previous generations of scholars have tended to believe. Economically all occupation sites, both fortified and unfortified, were apparently largely self-sufficient, and like others the occupants of forts had their own arable and pasture lands where they produced their cereal and meat. Thus with some notable exceptions we can look upon the hillforts as nucleated and defended rural communities. There are of course many outstanding questions concerning the nature, distribution and function of hillforts but for the purpose of our study they should be seen as complementary to the palisaded enclosures and undefended sites of the period.

During the Iron Age there were settlements or enclosures both fenced and some which were completely open, which appear with groupings of storage pits. Few of either sort have been extensively excavated in detail and we do not yet know how many houses we should assume were in any given enclosure, or how many pits are needed to imply the presence of a single house. Present evidence shows that fenced enclosures seem to have sheltered more than three or four houses. One would have expected there to have been larger villages or settlements, but it is not easy to produce convincing examples outside the forts. Nucleated settlements of village size seem to have continued in occupation into the Romano-British period, although it is very difficult to know how large they may have been in the Iron Age.

A number of extensive nucleated rural settlements of the later Iron Age have recently been investigated. Excavations at Little Waltham (Essex) indicate that there has been continuous occupation of the area since Neolithic times, its focus shifting within a radius of about 500 metres of the river crossing from time to time. Within the excavated area there is evidence of limited early prehistoric occupation which was confined to a scatter of residual artefacts together with a gully and hearth, probably dating from the Bronze Age. However, two successive pre-Belgic Iron Age settlements, the earlier open, the latter enclosed, were identified on the lower valley slopes. The open settlement adopted natural boundaries, a spring line on the south and a light natural dry valley to the north. The absence of stratification has made the interpretation of development difficult, but it would appear that the settlement was constantly evolving rather than changing dramatically at any given time. Casual finds point to a Belgic settlement to the south-east of the excavated site; a rich burial dating from AD 60–65 lay just to the south of the Roman road. During the Roman period at least three farms were sited on or near the road junction, one just east of the site; subsequently there appears to have been a break in occupation although late Saxon pottery has been found in Little Waltham village east of the river.

At Beckford in the Severn Valley north of Gloucester there

is a remarkable settlement of about three hectares comprising a series of individual ditch compounds, each with its own circular hut and pits for grain storage, rubbish and sewage. The houses here are circular in plan, and were built of small stakes set in a shallow groove except at the entrance where larger timber posts were inserted to carry the door. Each house possessed one or more clay-lined water tanks, and evidence recovered so far suggests that cereals were more important here than further west and that sheep and cattle were the main animals kept.

It is unrealistic to imagine a watertight division between the Iron Age and the Roman period – the subject of continuity is one which cannot be dealt with adequately here, but suffice to say that where evidence does survive it would appear to confirm the uninterrupted occupation of rural sites. At Woodcuts (Dorset) an Iron Age settlement began as a single farmstead and gradually developed into a village before it was finally abandoned in the late fourth century AD. Recent intensive work on the gravel terraced sites of the Upper Thames suggests that continuous occupation between the Iron Age and the Roman period is normal. At Carn Euny and Chysauster (Cornwall) occupation appears to have been continuous, if somewhat episodic, from the Iron Age onwards and even today habitation continues in the cottage adjacent to the reconstructed site. At Carn Euny, which is somewhat similar to Halangy Down on the Scilly Isles, there is no real regularity; instead a series of interlocking circles has house leading into house in a most chaotic fashion. The main plan of Carn Euny consists of three surviving courtyard houses with fine paved entrances, while the remains of at least four more stone houses were also found. Whether these were all of the large courtyard type or small single huts, such as the one near to the modern entrance to the site, is hard to tell. Underlying the stone-built villages there was an earlier phase of timber construction. Chysauster on the other hand has a much more regular layout, consisting of eight houses in a compact group of two rows, in use from the second century BC through to the third century AD (Plate X).

It is clear that in the past we have seriously underestimated the extent of Iron Age settlement in Britain; numerous new sites have emerged in the past few years, and in addition experiments in Iron Age farming techniques have brought about a reassessment of the capacity of Iron Age storage pits. Work at the Iron Age experimental farm site at Butser Hill (Hants) suggests that on the chalk at least the average storage pit appears to be capable of holding over forty bushels instead of four-and-a-half as had previously been thought. This means that the hundreds of pits found in association with many Iron Age and Romano-British sites must have been storage for cereals from a far larger agricultural area than was formerly imagined, and by inference, catering for a far greater rural population (Plate XI). Experiments with the cultivation of crops such as emmer and spelt also suggest that we have seriously underestimated the likely crop yields during the Iron Age. Although this work is still at an early stage it implies a fuller and better managed landscape than we had previously imagined. The implications for settlement studies are far reaching (see Fig. 14).

The concept of a considerable Iron Age population organized in estate groupings, whether associated with hill-forts or not, is one worthy of pursuit. There are substantial indications that by the late Iron Age the landscape in lowland Britain was covered with a pattern of villages, hamlets, and farmsteads already divided up into estates. This pattern was of course modified during the Roman period, but it remained substantially intact and emerged in the form of parish and estate boundaries in the late Saxon period, when the first credible written sources were compiled. Some scholars have further argued that in parts of central western Britain it is possible to identify sites which continued in occupation, perhaps as farmsteads, until the late Saxon period, and then formed the nucleus from which dependent townships developed during a period of population pressure and land hunger.

The Romano-British village

Apart from the study of villas, relatively little attention has been paid to rural settlement in Roman Britain. Convention-

69

ally settlement was often interpreted in terms of a pattern of munificent villas over much of lowland Britain, where the citizens lived in style, in stark contrast to the largely unlocated 'peasant sites' where the natives existed. The re-establishment of belief in the existence of villages in Roman Britain is a recent development and comes after a long period when it was thought that all peasant settlements were simple farmsteads. It is now accepted that social groups varied considerably in size and that many Iron Age communities passed unaltered into the Roman period.

It is quite clear that nucleated villages are to be found over much of lowland Britain during the Roman period. Several sites have provided evidence of planned streets and numerous platform houses, and range in size from one to ten hectares (Plate XII). It can be demonstrated that some of the villages occur in association with open or enclosed fields. A particularly good example of this is to be found at Thundersbarrow Hill (Sussex), where a considerable area of village and field earthworks lies next to a hillfort (see Fig. 12). The settlement developed in the late Iron Age alongside the ridgeway leading to the fort, and the fields spreading right up to the old ramparts. The site was occupied through to the fourth century and it is tempting to see the Romano-British villagers as the descendants of the hillfort community who first established themselves as early as the fifth century BC.

The term settlement has to be rather loosely applied to traces of Roman occupation that do not conform to the usual pattern of town, villa or isolated farmstead. Wherever detailed fieldwork is carried out such settlements are found to be common: for example, in the Gloucestershire Cotswolds four settlements of over ten hectares and more than forty of over four hectares have been located. At Eye Hall, Horningsea (Cambs) Roman occupation debris and kiln evidence extends over an area of 16.6 hectares, and at Ashton (Northants) occupation has been found over an area of five hectares. At Catsgore (Somerset) there is a five hectare settlement of several phases along a central trackway, while at Pinfold Lane, Castleton (Dorset), a Romano-British occupation covers a twenty hectare area; similar extensive undefined settlements

70

have been identified at Bush Marsh and Bawdrip and other Somerset sites. At Bulphan (Essex) a site covering six hectares was excavated in the last century and appears to have contained about twenty circular huts. Some of these must have been *vici*; the *vicus* was the smallest settlement unit recognized by the imperial authorities for the purpose of administration. This form of settlement is better understood on the continent where in certain areas of France and Germany the total settlement pattern of the Roman period is far clearer. A *vicus* could perhaps be compared with the small market towns of the Middle Ages: it often had a developed road system and public buildings as well as the right of electing its own magistrate.

The role and nature of the villa and its economy may not have been fully understood in the past. Instead of forming the sole unit of rural settlement as previously believed it is likely that the villas were only one part of the agrarian pattern, performing the function of a manor or country house. This means that the villas were simply the largest and most impressive of the rural dwellings, from whence the estates were managed. It is quite likely, however, that many villas had nucleated settlements associated with, if not actually attached to them. In the past excavations have tended to concentrate on the main structures of the villa and comparatively little attention has been paid to possible areas of outbuildings or extramural domestic occupation. There are growing indications that there were frequently village type communities associated with many villas, very much in the same way that medieval manors were attached to nucleated settlements.

Just how much did rural settlement continue unchanged during the first and second centuries AD? We do not have satisfactory evidence yet to answer this completely as the basis on which calculations can be made is inadequate. Certainly there were changes, new colonization was undertaken in some marginal areas – as has been most notably demonstrated in the Fenlands and the Pennines, where native villages developed in the second century to provide the army with grain. In some areas such as North Wales the evidence implies that deliberate rural colonization was a common feature. The emergence of a number of native villages and their field systems in the north

71

of England all developing at the same time indicates that the cultivation of oats as a summer crop may have been introduced as a result of the Roman corn levy. Similarly in the third century expansion of rural production and the native villages of the Pennines and Cumbria may date from a deliberate phase of colonization.

Some settlements, particularly the larger ones, were abandoned and replaced by an urban superstructure that often had quite a dramatic effect on the background rural settlement pattern. Similarly the construction of highly efficient road networks to service the army and later the cities must have polarized settlement growth along these arteries to some extent. The Roman conquest certainly added a major new element to the chemistry of settlement geography and quickened the normal process of settlement change in many areas. Nevertheless, the bare archaeological record which graphically demonstrates a change in the form of utensils may be deceiving us about the true nature of rural life over much of Roman Britain. The adoption of Roman artefacts does not necessarily imply an overall change in life style, and in many parts of the country rural settlement forms appear to have continued largely unchanged.

A distinctive feature of Romano–British villages is that many of them contain elements of industrial activity. Pottery production and iron working appears to have been the principal activity in some rural settlements. On the Mendips substantial evidence of Roman mining has been located, and often the associated settlements appear to have been operating village fields. No doubt there were hamlets associated with other forms of extractive industry in other parts of Britain during the Roman period, but relatively little work has been carried out to identify them.

Despite the fact that many towns lying over Roman settlements have inherited features such as streets and defence alignments, few topographical features in our villages are of Roman origin. At Dorchester on Thames (Oxon) and Leintwardine (Hereford & Worcester) villages occupy the sites of Roman towns and the line of the Roman defences has partially survived, but at Dorchester the plan of the modern settlement comes from a small market community which developed outside the medieval abbey gates (see Fig. 10). It is true that a number of linear villages such as Fenny Stratford (Bucks) have developed along the line of Roman roads, but the origins of the roads seems to be largely irrelevant as the villages are late Saxon or medieval. Caxton (Cambs) is a linear village spread out along Ermine Street, but the original settlement appears to have been around the church which lies a quarter of a mile to the south-west of the Roman road. Similarly few Roman names for rural settlements are in current use; far more frequent is the use of the place-name element 'chester' or 'caster', which derives from *ceaster* (Old English), and denotes Anglo-Saxon recognition of a Roman settlement or fort.

Fieldwork investigation in various parts of the country has demonstrated that nucleated rural settlement was ubiquitous in Roman Britain. One of the remarkable features to emerge from recent rescue excavations is just how commonly Romano-British material is recovered from in or close by modern villages. There appears to be considerable variety in the forms of village, hamlets and farmsteads throughout the country, and only intense local work can identify the detailed pattern of rural settlement. Let us examine three areas, the north-east, Wessex and the Fenlands, where intensive fieldwork has revealed something of the complexity of the Romano-British village.

The north-east

In Northumberland and Durham unenclosed settlements of round stone-built houses are quite common during the Roman period. These communities frequently overlie the abandoned defences of Iron Age forts, particularly in the border country, but although they sometimes show clear signs of continuity they often appear to be purely Roman settlements set within a pattern of Celtic fields which they were obviously utilizing. Some of the settlements contain scooped enclosures which are believed to belong to earlier phases. Other sites, such as Coldmouth Hill (Northumb) contain traces of circular platforms on which stood timber-built huts, while others contain secondary stone-built huts. Although all the dwellings in the smaller settlements could have been contemporary it looks as though the larger settlements developed gradually by additions to an original homestead. This has suggested to some scholars that these homesteads may represent the fragmentation of groups which formerly occupied the hillforts into that area which was once defended by the fort.

Most of the settlements are quite small, consisting of about six huts, but Greeves Bash (Northumb) in the Cheviot foothills contains some forty surviving stone huts. At Brans Hill (Northumb) there are a dozen settlements scattered along one-and-a-half kilometres of hill-slope, and in a two-mile stretch of the Bremish Valley there are a hundred and fifty huts contained within numerous enclosures. The basic form of these settlements consists of a stone-walled enclosure which is oval or circular in form. This contains a varying number of huts fronting onto a yard which in some cases has been scooped below the level of the dwelling area; it may have been necessary to construct steps between the yard and the houses. The yards are in some cases roughly paved and their hollowed nature resembles more recent farm stockyards which have seen long use (Fig. 15). Generally the sites are similar to those found in the Pennines or Wales.

The dwellings are in the form of circular stone-built huts which are on average six metres in diameter. Some contain traces of internal partitions but in most cases there is little evidence of separate rooms. Similarly, apart from the occasional grouping of huts in pits, one large, one small, there is little indication of social difference within the community. At Huckhoe (Northumb) traces of internal wattled partitions were found during excavations. In some cases rectangular stone buildings of the later Roman period have been identified but these are exceptional.

Some of the enclosures are rectilinear and contain stone-built structures, sometimes with a shallow outer ditch which appears to have been for drainage rather than defence. These enclosures contain four or five round stone huts fronting onto two cobbled yards, separated by a paved causeway leading to

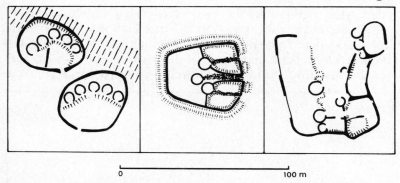

15. Prehistoric villages in Northumberland (after Jobey 1966).

the dwelling area; sometimes they contained subsidiary wooden buildings. There is little trace of expansion outside the enclosures whatever their shape and they appear to be regularly distributed about the countryside when they are found. This has led some writers to suggest that they may represent colonizing settlements for agricultural purposes during the second and third centuries AD.

Wessex

The archaeology of the chalk downlands of south-western Britain has been studied for a considerable length of time. Fieldwork on prehistoric earthworks dates from at least the eighteenth century, but it is only in recent times that any attempt has been made to complete the information to provide a satisfactory analysis of ancient settlement patterns. In Wiltshire and Dorset work undertaken by the Royal Commission on Historic and Ancient Monuments and others has identified a large number of earthworks belonging to Roman villages. Romano-British settlement in this area is almost always associated with a road which runs through the village or close to it. These roads often funnel out into an open space of up to a quarter of a hectare at one end or by the side of the settlement; such open areas might serve a communal function, for a market or for herding animals, very much in the style of the

75

later village green. In the case of Meriden Down (Dorset) which lies in the parish of Winterborne Halton at a height of about 200 metres, the nucleus of the settlement (1.4 hectares) is bounded by a bank and external ditch to the north-west and south-west (Fig. 16). The centre is covered by a levelled

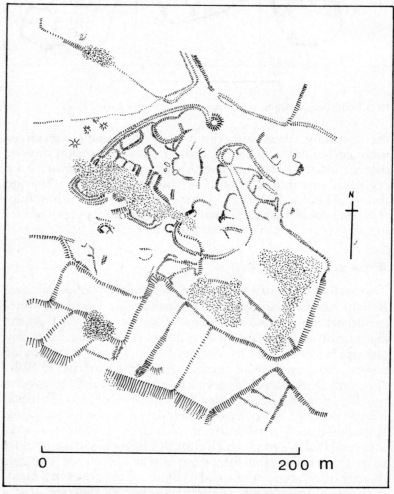

16. A well-preserved prehistoric settlement site and field system at Meriden Down, Dorset (After R.C.H.M.).

platform and embanked area which indicates the sites of structures and working areas. Three embanked loops, presumably the compounds around three larger buildings, project southwards on the south side of a medieval park, and four roads lead to an open space immediately outside the settlement. There is no evidence here for expansion outside the original nucleus. There is another contemporary settlement less than half a mile to the south, and signs of other settlements on this ridge where an ancient way led towards Hod Hill to the north and southwards towards a possible junction with the Roman road to Dorchester (Dorset). Such fragments help to show that in Wessex, and over most of the chalk downlands, there was for at least most of the Roman period a permanent pattern of nucleated settlements of varying status connected to each other by roads. In many instances this produced an ancillary network of communications.

Some of the settlements are of considerable size. Town Hill in the parish of Frampton (Dorset) covers at least two-and-a-half hectares, while Chiselbury Warren (Wilts) covers six hectares. Here we seem to have some evidence for the existence of a linear street village of the Roman period. A central street runs for about 600 metres and along it lie a number of rectangular platforms, a few of them being 18 metres in length but most of them measuring up to 30 metres. There is a junction of roads towards the east end where the existing building sites may have filled in a former small open area, and at the west end a number of terraced tracks skirt a markedly triangular open space. Celtic fields are visible to the northwest and the north, their regularity adding to the impression that they were laid out in the Roman period. Adjacent to the settlement on the south-east is a large but indefinable area of badly damaged Celtic fields of the more usual irregular appearance.

At the south-west side of Salisbury Plain, on Knoock Down near Warminster (Wilts), are two other settlements arranged along streets. The western settlement covers some eight hectares and is made up of a large number of rectangular platforms. The eastern settlement is three hectares in extent and has fewer houses, more widely spaced, mostly in large rectangular ditched compounds arranged on either side as a sunken street running north to south. Surface finds indicate that both settlements were occupied in the Roman period. An interesting feature of Knoock Down West is the presence of a triangular open space of about 0.2 hectares, which has the outward appearance of a medieval village green. Similar open spaces at road junctions have been identified on other Wessex earthwork sites. These are usually smaller than greens but since there is normally only one in any community it is probable that they belonged to the community as whole and not the nearest house. Quite apart from these newly found Roman villages, it has been suggested that on Fyfield Down (Wilts) some areas of earthworks may represent that same type of Romano-British colonization as has been indicated in the north-east. We can therefore see that some of the Wessex settlements are of sufficient size and contain an adequate number of platforms to deserve to be called villages. Their plans are nearer those of some medieval villages than anything recognizable as such during the prehistoric period, but on the whole their associated fields are in the Celtic tradition.

The Roman fenlands

Finally we move to another area where there has been intensive fieldwork in recent years – the Fenlands. Here it is suggested that in the area around the Wash the majority of some three hundred sites of the Roman period were nucleated in a number of different ways, some of them being clearly regular villages while others represent component sites. The investigation which has produced this evidence combined meticulous field observation with the use of aerial photography.

Around AD 50 as a result of a general relative lowering of the sea level, the area surrounding the Wash in the northern part of Cambridgeshire emerged from the sea so that extensive tidal mud flats became silt lines just above tide level. Tidal water was confined to a multitude of winding channels traversing the former estuary. The higher dry areas formed along these channels became suitable sites for settlement while rich silt provided potential arable land. The result was that within a few years colonization began, and in the first part of the second century AD there was a massive and possibly centrally organized settlement all over the silt lands. Dozens of new villages, hamlets and farmsteads surrounded by fields and paddocks appeared. Much of the colonization appears to have been associated with an apparently contemporary system of lodes or navigable canals which link the chalkland with the River Cam. One of the interesting features to emerge from this research is that in most cases nucleation appears to have been the result of organic development and not conscious planning from the subdivision of the family holdings. The original settlement unit appears to have been based on kinship groups leading to the development of secondary hamlets.

This massive colonization of the silt Fens was not completely successful. Many sites were abandoned before AD 200 and archaeological evidence indicates a constant battle against flooding and bad drainage – parts of the newly colonized area were subsequently totally inundated by sea once more. The remainder, however, survived and were occupied until at least the early fifth century and probably later. On the Fen edge in Cambridgeshire at least two sites survive in earthwork form, one at Cottenham (Plates XIII and XIV) and one at Chittering, where blocks of continuous sub-rectangular enclosures in which the houses appear to have stood are bounded by wide drainage channels.

The full extent of Romano-British rural settlement has yet to be determined, and over much of the lowland zone the settlement pattern may have been effectively masked by subsequent development. However, wherever detailed fieldwork has been undertaken, both in upland and lowland areas, tantalizing evidence of extensive Roman occupation has been found. Some scholars suggest that a pattern of nucleated villages and estates was established in the late Iron Age as a result of population pressure and that this pattern survived in modified form until the seventh or eighth century AD. Such conjecture remains to be proved on a large scale, but the clues that are emerging should be enough to warn us of the danger of accepting any dogmatic assumptions about the nature of Romano-British rural settlement.

Villages in the landscape

SELECT BIBLIOGRAPHY

Branigan, K. and Fowler, P., *The Roman West Country* (1976).

Cunliffe, B., *Iron Age Communities in Britain* (1974).

Fowler, P. J. (ed.), *Recent Work in Rural Archaeology* (1975).

Hallam, S. J., 'Villages in Roman Britain: Some Evidence', *Antiquaries Journal*, 44 (1964).

Harding, D. W., *The Iron Age in the Upper Thames Basin* (1972).

Harding, D. W. (ed.), *Hillforts* (1976).

Phillips, C. W. (ed.), *The Fenland in Roman Times* (1970).

Taylor, C., *Fields in the Landscape* (1975).

Thomas, A. C. (ed.), *Rural Settlement in Roman Britain*, CBA, Research Report No. 7 (1966).

VII The twin churches of St Mary and SS Gyriac and Julia at Swaffham Prior provide an unusual testimony of individual piety or rivalry between local lords. It is not known who was responsible for these two foundations.

VIII   Multi-period occupation site dating from the Neolithic to the Viking at Jarlshof, Shetland.

IX   The hillfort at Caer Caradoc, Shropshire. Many such sites were probably occupied by village communities in the Iron Age.

X   Prehistoric and native British courtyard houses of the village of Chysauster, Cornwall.

XI The excavated remains of an Iron Age hut circle, at Abingdon, Oxfordshire, on the gravel terrace of the River Thames. The gulleys represent either the foundation trench for the hut walls or an outside trench dug for drainage purposes. This was one of a series of such huts, probably a village settlement. The pits in the background were principally for grain storage.

XII Native settlement at Ewe Close, Cumbria. The aerial photograph shows an enclosed village of half a hectare with an eastern extension of irregular stone-walled enclosures.

4　The villages of Anglo-Saxon England

The migration and Anglo-Saxon period conventionally lasts from the time of the arrival of the first Germanic migrants at the end of the fourth century AD to the Norman Conquest of 1066. As with all archaeological terms of a generic nature they mask enormous diversity, and within these seven centuries there was considerable typological and regional variation in settlement form and pattern in Britain. They were also centuries which saw enormous changes in culture, economy and population. This discussion is limited largely to England and includes little evidence from the 'Celtic West', Norse settlements or fringe areas where the use of the term 'Anglo-Saxon' is in any case questionable.

As we move into the post-Roman period the problems of rural settlement become increasingly complex. The settlement historian seeking to identify early Anglo-Saxon 'villages' is faced with enormous difficulties. It is a period for which we have a progressively well-rehearsed historical narrative, together with a deeply ingrained scholarly tradition which is strengthened as it incorporates the very making of the English landscape. To counter this we have a bewildering array of facts and theories resulting from recent research, many of them apparently contradictory, but all united in their opposition to traditional beliefs about the Anglo-Saxon settlement. We should now be less confident about the form of early Anglo-Saxon rural settlement than about Iron Age farmsteads or Romano-British villas. Despite, or perhaps because of, increasing research into this period, our concepts about the distribution, social and geographical form and the relationship of the new communities to already existing settlements are all extremely imprecise. Consequently, archaeologists, geographers and place-name historians have all seriously questioned the concept of the Anglo-Saxon 'invasion' together with its related settlements.

It is ironic that early Saxon settlements should prove to be elusive. Until recently it was firmly believed that it was just these incoming Teutons who brought with them the English village and established the fundamental pattern of English settlement. It was thought that the 'invaders' – groups of free English settlers – gradually quelled native Romano-British or Celtic opposition, took over their agricultural land and established clearly defined nucleated villages, and then moved on to the task of clearing the still extensive tracts of primeval woodland, in the process of creating new villages and hamlets. It was even suggested that ethnic differences among the tribes of incoming settlers accounted for variations in the morphology and pattern of villages in different parts of eastern England. It was admitted that in western Britain and in pockets throughout the rest of the country some native occupation survived, but it was generally accepted that the Saxons created the fabric of English rural society – a fabric that had largely survived into the twentieth century. These beliefs were based upon straightforward observation of surviving settlements, the accounts of early historians, the analysis of place-names, inference from the continental evidence and the rather badly digested evidence from the excavation of pagan Saxon burial grounds.

In north-west Europe, particularly on the northern seaboard of Germany, modern village plans conform to well-defined patterns, such as 'green villages', lying around circular, square or rectangular open spaces, 'street villages', strung out along a length of road, and 'crossroad villages', sited at the junction of two or more routeways. The arrangement of these villages with their regular streets and internal boundaries suggested a high degree of planning at the time when the settlements were conceived. Added to this many English village plans, particularly those in north-eastern Britain, appeared to conform to the German pattern, which enabled them to be readily classified under the same system.

Scholars, working on the basis of village plans depicted on post-medieval maps, projected those forms backwards a thousand years and believed that they closely resembled the original settlements.

The apparent antiquity of these settlement forms, in the eyes of the scholars, was reinforced by the findings of archaeological excavations in north-western mainland Europe. These have demonstrated that villages with regular plans similar to those of modern settlements existed during the period of the Roman Empire. It was therefore argued that these forms were brought across the Channel by the north Europeans when they came to England. At *Warendorf* and *Feddersen Wierde* in Germany and *Kootwijk* and *Wijster* in Holland, for example, successive phases of compact communities have been excavated, and have been found to be village settlements consisting of timber-framed farmsteads, ancillary buildings, workshops, property and precinct boundaries, pits and wells. The displaced inhabitants of *Wijster*, which continued in existence into the fifth century AD, could well have migrated to England, where we might legitimately have expected them and their descendants to have built similar types of dwellings, established a similar settlement layout and operated a similar economy. Finally, as the majority of English villages carry Anglo-Saxon place-names the argument seemed irrefutable. It was obvious that these village forms were introduced by the incoming settlers and survived with little change into the Middle Ages and with some modification through to the present day.

These arguments do however contain a fundamental flaw – there is no evidence to show that our modern villages were laid down by the early Saxons. For such a non-literate period only the archaeological record can be expected to provide conclusive proof of the Anglo-Saxon origins of our villages. The accumulated evidence is not conclusive but does demonstrate three aspects of rural settlement, all of them at variance with the conventional story. Firstly there are indications already mentioned, that the basic framework of rural settlement is far older than Saxon, and possibly prehistoric. Secondly, hardly any early nucleated Anglo-Saxon villages have been found and

83

the absence of early or mid Saxon occupation levels from excavated deserted villages undermines the probability of their Saxon origins. Finally, it is obvious that there is considerable settlement mobility at all times and that many of the village shapes we perceive today, both regular and irregular, came into being in the Middle Ages or later.

There is a growing body of evidence to support the view that although the end of Roman Britain brought about the collapse of urban life and the disintegration of most of the institutions associated with imperial rule, there was a considerable degree of continuity in rural areas. The nature of this continuity is still a question of some controversy, but it seems most likely that the incoming settlers were far less numerous than has conventionally been thought. Also, the process of migration took place over a very long period and although there may have been considerable upheaval in some places, generally speaking the incoming Saxons either settled alongside indigenous farmers or occupied areas that had not previously been intensively cultivated. This is no doubt a simplistic picture of what must have been a highly complicated and prolonged process, but it conforms more accurately to the available evidence than the old model of a cataclysmic holocaust.

It can no longer be assumed that because a village has an Anglo-Saxon place-name it was necessarily founded during that period. It may originally have had a Celtic or even earlier name, as do many natural features such as rivers and woods, and the Saxon name could have been grafted on, perhaps several centuries later. It has recently been convincingly argued that in western and parts of central England the Saxon conquest was primarily political and not a folk movement and as such simply replaced the aristocracy, in which case it is probable that the English language took several centuries to become vernacular. For many years the indigenous population would have been bilingual and English may only have become dominant in the late Saxon period with increased political control and the spread of administrative literacy. The name Walton (O.E. *wealh* or *walh tun*) and Bretton (O.E. *Brettas*) may relate to communities of Welshmen or indigenous Britons. Although the place-name element 'Wal' cannot automatically be linked with native survival, there are some interesting examples, for instance at Fotheringhay (Northants) there are a considerable number of prehistoric and Romano-British sites including a large Roman settlement visible in cropmark form, associated with a villa whose modern name is Walcote Lodge, i.e. 'cote of the Britons or serfs'. Several names on our maps today must have originated at a time when English settlers formed a minority among a predominantly Celtic-speaking population. Pensax (Worcs) is a Welsh name meaning 'hill of the Saxons', and Englebourne (Devon) is 'the stream of the English'.

In western England Saxon domination was not achieved until the late seventh or eighth century AD. Thus for up to 300 years these areas remained Romano–British or even Celtic. If we assume that there was no widespread folk movement westwards in the mid Saxon period, there is absolutely no reason to suppose that the settlement pattern we see in 1086 was Saxon at all. For example, in south Shropshire we have a group of manors – Clun, Clunbury, Clungunford and Clunton – all of which have a Celtic or pre-Celtic river-name as a prefix and a Saxon suffix. Here, surely, we are looking at a very ancient pattern of settlement, where the names have simply been partly Anglicized.

The incidence of early Saxon material found in association with Roman occupation is impressive. The land occupied by early Saxon settlements was often closely associated with Roman towns or estates. Roman finds are often numerous and closely associated with Saxon finds and buildings. In the past such finds have been dismissed as residual but it seems more than likely that they represent substantial contact and cooperation with late Roman groups. Some 15 per cent of known Roman sites in Wiltshire can be shown to have Saxon evidence associated with them. A considerable number of churches in the Cotswolds and elsewhere lie on or very near to Roman villas. For example at Hinton St Mary and Fifehead (Dorset), Roman villas, both of which have provided evidence of Christianity, lie close to the church and later village.

There is cumulative evidence from excavated sites such as Barton Court, near Abingdon (Oxon) that the major break in the sequence of settlement comes not at the end of Roman occupation, but in the middle or late Saxon period. Much of this evidence is, however, not conclusive – the superimposition of Saxon above Roman levels is not necessarily proof of continuity of community or even of habitation; more convincing perhaps is the work on estate boundaries. Professor Finberg in a pioneer study demonstrated that at Withington (Glos) the agricultural estates operated through from the late Roman period into the Saxon age without a break. Since then there have been a number of other studies to show the same phenomena in other parts of the country.

Perhaps the most persuasive arguments are, however, negative ones. The incoming settlers were essentially farmers, who brought no radically new farming techniques with them. As far as we can see they operated a mixed agrarian economy and used Celtic fields very much in the traditional way. There is no conceivable reason therefore why they should have destroyed a functioning system and then replaced it with a facsimile of the original. Added to this is the scarcity of Anglo-Saxon material and structures from deserted medieval villages where excavation has taken place. Here surely is the perfect opportunity to trace the origins of the village back to its early Saxon foundation. Almost without exception this has proved to be illusory – even at Wharram Percy (N. Yorks) where two areas of early Saxon occupation have now been found, one to the north-east and one well to the south of the medieval village, it is quite clear that these settlements have little or nothing to do with the later village, which appears to have been laid out just before the Norman Conquest. Excavations of deserted medieval villages have demonstrated that the vast majority of nucleated villages did not originate in the early Saxon period, although recent work at Goltho (Lincs) and Barton Blount (Derby) indicates that evidence of nucleated communities of the mid and late Saxon period could be quite common.

The nature of Anglo-Saxon settlement

What then is the nature of the evidence available for the study of English settlement and more particularly the types of communities and houses in which the settlers and their descendants lived? There are few documentary sources of value to the settlement historian for this period, much of the narrative history being written at a later date, and the few contemporary sources include little detailed information about settlements. The histories and the Anglo-Saxon Chronicle tell us virtually nothing about the form or pattern of early settlement, and as a source for the geography of the period can be positively misleading. Even the evidence from the Domesday Book (1086), which has conventionally been regarded as portraying the evolved Saxon landscape, has to be handled with the greatest care. It is now quite clear that the Domesday record is a deceptive guide to settlement patterns. Until recently it was generally assumed that the Domesday Manor was a single nucleated community. This belief is no longer valid as we know that a single Domesday manorial assessment could cover a large number of settlements, including isolated farmsteads.

Occasionally, there are hints – for instance in the late seventh century St Cuthbert records staying in a place called Hruringaham, apparently somewhere near Melrose, when a house at the east end of the village caught fire, and as the wind was blowing strongly from that direction it looked as if the whole village would be destroyed. The saint brought about a change of the wind by his prayers and thus saved the settlement. Here there appears to be a clear reference to a nucleated village community. Some pictorial representations of dwellings and settlements survive, the most notable example being the Bayeux Tapestry where eleventh-century buildings of various classes are depicted, mainly as single cell structures. Similarly, in the tenth-century ordinances it is assumed that all men belong to a village (villa or *tunscipe*). However, such references rarely provide a detailed picture of a complete settlement, and in any case date from several centuries after the original Saxon settlement.

Place-name evidence has been widely used in the past. It was believed that the chronology of the English settlement could be traced through the examination of Anglo-Saxon place-name elements. For instance, the elements *ing* and *ham* represented the first phase of the settlement and *ton* was indicative of later colonization. This view can no longer be accepted and it is clear that although place-names can assist in the study they must be used cautiously. The place-name element *ham* is of particular importance meaning 'a village, a village community, an estate, a manor, a homestead'. It appears, like its continental counterpart *heim*, to be closely associated with areas of former Roman occupation; great care should be taken in using this element, however, as it can be confused with *hamm*. Recent research has indicated that the suffix *hamm* can have at least eight separate meanings and, to understand the true origin, each place must be studied individually. In the south-eastern counties of England there has been detailed work on the relationship between *ham* names, Romano-British sites and roads and pagan Saxon cemeteries. Generally speaking *ham* names are either on a Roman road or at a discrete distance from one, suggesting that these names were given when districts which had developed in Roman times, and areas immediately adjacent, were being occupied by the English. The relevance of a Roman background is particularly clear in the Darenth Valley (Kent) where the *ham* names are close to Roman villa sites. This is an area where there is evidence of continuous occupation of territory and land use, whereas the habitations change, the Romano-British villa sites being replaced by a neighbouring *ham*.

A comparison of the distribution of *ham* names with that of pagan cemeteries indicates that while generally they do not coincide, at the fringe of the pagan burial districts there is a fair degree of overlap. Furthermore this research has shown that in the south-east *ham* preceded the formation of *ingas/inga* names but continued in use at the same time. The distribution of the *ham* type suggests that it came into use at the very beginning of a colonization phase during which the Anglo-Saxons moved beyond the initial immigration areas and during which they began to take over land within, on the edge of, and beyond the districts which had been occupied and developed in Roman times. In the south-east the *ham* names record a process taking place in the fifth and sixth centuries; it can also be demonstrated that a similar process occurred in Cheshire during the seventh century. To be of further assistance in the study of Anglo-Saxon settlement, place-name studies must obviously take the form of detailed local examinations, such as the recent analysis of *Wicham* names which relates them to roads and to the Roman *vicus* settlements. As has already been indicated, the greatest danger in the use of such evidence is confusing the dynamics of place-names and geography with the physical realities of a changing settlement pattern.

Our prime source of information is archaeological – until comparatively recently work in this period has concentrated upon the identification and excavation of burial grounds. As these sites are far easier to find, and are ostensibly more rewarding to examine, this is not surprising. Nonetheless, this work has led to an imbalance in our understanding of the early Saxons. Some archaeologists assumed that the settlements which were associated with the cemeteries lay under extant villages or were covered by soil drift and in some cases this is no doubt true. However, the assumption that burials were automatically closely associated with settlements has been questioned by some fieldworkers who suggest that cemeteries might have been placed close to estate or territorial boundaries, a common practice used to confirm or enforce the delineation of a boundary. Added to this is the evidence of place-names mentioned above which suggests that the settlements may have lain some distance from the cemeteries. In recent years a considerable number of early and middle Saxon grave groups have proved to be relatively small, consisting of no more than half a dozen inhumations, indicating the presence of much smaller communities, perhaps isolated farmsteads over large areas of countryside.

Before we examine the evidence from excavations we must look at the field evidence. Although virtually no standing vernacular building of any substance survives from the Saxon period, we do have a considerable number of stone-built churches whose fabric dates wholly or partially from before the Norman Conquest. The structure of the church will often reflect the prosperity of the community it served, and its position may help in the elucidation of settlement history in relation to the surviving associated villages. The church of St

89

Mary at Deerhurst (Glos) for instance, has been shown to incorporate many Saxon phases; the village is now scattered, but it is possible that there was once a considerable community there, possibly clustered around or close to the church. In those settlements where there is a Saxon church it would be valuable to study the street pattern and general settlement form in relationship to the church. Recent attention to fabric of Saxon churches and the archaeology of the surrounding area at key sites such as Repton (Derby) and Brixworth (Northants) is likely to be extremely informative.

There are few if any identifiable earthworks of Saxon villages. This is largely due to the fact that the vast majority of Saxon buildings were of timber, turf or clay and therefore when abandoned left little trace. Only occasionally do we find evidence of the use of stone in vernacular Saxon buildings. The earthworks which may have derived from property boundaries or roadways would have been built over or ploughed out. Those which do survive from the Saxon period tend to be of the massive linear variety, such as Offa's Dyke or Wansdyke and, as such, have so far contributed little to understanding contemporary settlement although some recent research in East Anglia suggests that it might just be possible to relate phases of settlement history to such linear boundaries.

The identification of Saxon sites by aerial reconnaissance has proved difficult in the past. Recently, however, some possible sites have been identified such as the characteristic markings of sunken huts at Mucking (Essex). Plate XV shows the rectangular buildings of a possible middle Saxon settlement at Drayton (Oxon). As we learn to recognize the principal surviving features more easily the value of aerial survey will undoubtedly increase, and some sites which have previously been interpreted as prehistoric or Romano-British may in fact prove to be Saxon.

The application of fieldwalking to Saxon settlement has been most impressive. At North Elmham (Norfolk) intense field survey has enabled the reconstruction of the middle and late Saxon settlement patterns. Similarly, work of part-time fieldwalkers consolidated by the Royal Commission on Historical Monuments in Northamptonshire has produced evidence of six or seven Saxon 'settlements' per modern parish. Admittedly these sites are often represented by a single sherd or a scatter of sherds, but it is a pattern that is repeatedly found and the implications concerning the nature of Saxon settlements are far reaching. In areas where Saxon pottery can readily be found on the surface such studies are likely to be of major importance.

If we cannot accept the traditional concept of the early Saxon village, what then are the chief characteristics of the settlements that have been identified? The answer is equivocal. We do not know if the scattered traces of early Saxon rural settlement which have been found really represent a complete picture of Saxon settlement at all. It is possible that many of the identified settlements represent isolated farmsteads, habitations of bands of mercenary soldiers or farmworkers rather than organized village groups. If this is the case we may well be dealing with an extremely mixed settlement pattern, reminiscent of the Roman and pre-Roman periods, when in some areas the village is the exception rather than the rule.

Most of the sites investigated have been in response to a threat of destruction – normally from sand and gravel working. It therefore follows that most of the known sites that qualify as 'villages' tend to lie on the lighter soils on river terraces, where the possibility of identification by aerial photograph or by chance as a result of mineral extraction is much higher. This, of course, gives us a biased sample from the beginning. Despite the fact that traces of early Saxon buildings have now been found in well over a hundred localities, the accumulated evidence is still inconclusive. Most of the sites which have received attention have been only partially excavated and no one site has, at the time of writing, been completely investigated. In most cases only one or two structures have been identified, and many others do not appear to have formed part of a nucleated settlement. We therefore have an insufficient number of settlement plans to enable a realistic chronological analysis; added to this we are faced with a considerable degree of ambiguity concerning the nature of the surviving traces of the buildings themselves.

By far the most commonly found structure of the early

Saxon period is the sunken floored building or *grübenhaus*. These are found in the form of shallow rectangular or oval scoops, normally with one or more post-holes at either end. When they were constructed, an excavation was made into the ground to an average depth of 0.50 to 0.75 metres. The hollows were often dug into the subsoil and after they were abandoned the depressions filled with topsoil, thus they are easily identifiable as well-defined darker patches cut into the natural subsoil. Such buildings are first found in early Germanic contexts of the late fourth and early fifth centuries and are clearly derived from their continental counterparts. They are a common feature of most but not all English settlements of the early period; they continue to appear less frequently on middle and late Saxon sites.

There is considerable disagreement about the nature of the buildings which these structures represent. It is argued by some that they were simply roofed by a tent-like timber frame, covered with reeds or thatch and were thus basically rough crude dwellings – a reconstruction to this format can be seen at the West Dean Museum of Rural Life in Sussex. This viewpoint was best expressed by E. T. Leeds who, when working at Sutton Courtenay (Oxon), was one of the first archaeologists to recognize sunken-floored buildings. On the basis of his discoveries there he wrote 'The bulk of the people, we can now be assured, were content with something that hardly deserves a title better than hovel, only varying in its greater or lesser simplicity'. The presence of hearths on the floors of some sunken huts led Leeds at least to believe that these 'cabins' were the normal houses of the incoming Saxon settlers who dwelled 'with bare head-room, amid a filthy litter of broken bones, food and shattered pottery, with logs or planks raised on stones for their seats or couches . . .' and indeed the excavated evidence from many similar sites would appear to confirm this view. As late as 1948 a survey on the Anglo-Saxons concluded that 'The invaders were for the most part in a culturally primitive condition . . . their habitations were so wretchedly flimsy – a rectangular scraping in the ground with wattle walls and a thatched roof seems to have been the limit of their known architectural competence.'

It is now, however, very difficult to accept this viewpoint. The 'evidence' of squalor and primitive techniques is at variance with the craftsmanship and technical mastery seen in contemporary artefacts. Where carpentry techniques can be studied, as at the recently discovered late Saxon water mill at Tamworth (Staffs), the craftsmanship is shown to be of a very high quality, and indeed it is far from certain that the sunken-floored buildings were squalid hovels. Reconstruction of these structures suggests that they could be quite spacious and extremely comfortable. Similarly the evidence from the stone churches implies a far higher standard of architecture than is indicated by the underground archaeological evidence, and many of the architectural features of the stone churches appear to have derived from earlier wooden edifices.

The excavation of Saxon royal palaces at Yeavering (Northumb) and Cheddar (Somerset) has clearly shown that the Saxons were capable of building highly sophisticated wooden structures. One of the most obvious discrepancies, however, is the radical difference between sunken-floored buildings and those structures of the same period found on the continent. Most contemporary north European settlements consisted of one or more large halls, often of the 'three aisled long-house' or of the *Warendorf* type, each with appropriate ancillary buildings. It is perhaps significant that in such a context the sunken-floored structure is rarely a dwelling, but much more often a workshop or store. At *Wijster* near Beilen in Holland large-scale excavations have produced a series of buildings within the long-house tradition and have revealed in detail the plan and development of an associated settlement and cemetery on an extensive inland site. The excavations have provided plans of 86 major buildings and 167 sunken-floored buildings. *Wijster* is just one of the many settlements which was deserted at the very time when the transfer of traditions of settlement layout, building design and carpentry from the north-west European coastlands to England should have taken place. Some scholars have also pointed out that literary evidence refers to substantial buildings, most notably in *Beowulf* where we hear of great hall-buildings.

The presence of loom weights on the floor of many

sunken-floored huts suggested to some archaeologists that they may have been workshops and that the associated post-hole and sill-beam buildings occasionally found in British sites, had been destroyed. Leeds himself did identify traces of more ambitious rectangular hall-like buildings at Sutton Courtenay, which he dismissed as being of later date. Aerial reconnaissance has also provided evidence of possible long-halls in the vicinity. There are even grounds to believe that the sunken-floored buildings were arranged around a large open space.

Alternatively the sunken-floored buildings have been inter-preted as barns, byres, storehouses, bakehouses, pottery workshops or granaries. The presence of large quantities of animal bones has suggested to others that the early buildings may not have been permanently occupied but were either the temporary dwellings of nomadic pastoralists or occupied only seasonally, as part of a pattern of transhumance. Other archaeologists believe that they were boarded over and that the hollows formed cellars. It has also been convincingly argued that in some cases such cellars were only component parts of larger buildings, and the associated structural post-holes or sill-beams have not been identified or have been destroyed. Nevertheless the question of the sunken-floored buildings remains something of an enigma, and it is just these structures which provide much of the information for the buildings of the early Saxon period.

Unlike many of the European sites most of the Saxon settlements which have been investigated in England have not been waterlogged or protected by a covering of peat or sand. Consequently, the evidence from post-hole and timber-slot buildings is far more elusive because it is more susceptible to destruction. This does not mean, however, that these struc-tures were necessarily slight or ephemeral. Some of the most telling evidence has come from excavations at West Stow in Suffolk. The arrangement of this settlement conforms much more closely to contemporary European patterns, but the extraordinary circumstances of its preservation have meant that it has yielded far more information than many other sites. Here an early Saxon village, founded before the end of the

Roman period during the late fourth century has been examined in detail (Fig. 17). It was ploughed for a period during the early Middle Ages, and then apparently covered over and protected by sand in the thirteenth century. It is true that an area of only two-and-a-half hectares has been examined, but West Stow does currently provide the most convincing evidence from an early nucleated Saxon community in England.

Some six halls were occupied at one time or another during the fifth and sixth centuries, each with one or more sunken huts associated with it. The halls were substantial post-built rectangular structures, but unlike continental examples, they were not divided into living and animal quarters. This may reflect a difference in economy or environment. Other structures seem to represent outhouses, workshops and sheds and some buildings appear to have been common to the village as a whole. The arrangement of the buildings into apparently

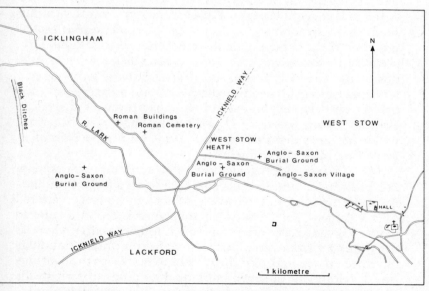

17.   Settlement migration along the River Lark at West Stow, Suffolk (after Scarfe 1972).

associated units related to a common central area accords well with the type of settlement one might reasonably expect from the incoming settlers. There was a system of boundary ditches at West Stow which suggests that the original settlement was laid out according to some kind of plan; these boundaries did not, however, survive into the later phase of the village. This indicates a flexibility of property boundaries that is constantly repeated in the discoveries from later deserted medieval villages.

The settlement at West Stow suggests a small community of perhaps no more than three or four families at any one time. Each family probably occupied a hall with its associated outhouses, workshops and sheds. Despite the absence of permanent internal boundaries the relative distance apart of the main structure does suggest some lasting internal arrangement. No evidence of associated fields has been identified, but animal bones show that sheep raising and wool working formed an important part of the economy. Like many contemporary settlements the site was abruptly but not violently abandoned in the mid seventh century. Apart from some burnt weaving sheds there were no signs of disaster; it would appear that at this time the inhabitants deliberately moved to another site, possibly in the vicinity of the present village about a mile upstream. The early Saxon site at West Stow is only one of a sequence of sites in the immediate area, and it has been argued that the small hamlet here simply occupied a vacant niche in an already existing settlement framework. There is no other site which has provided such positive evidence for the plan of an early English hamlet (Fig. 17).

The other major excavation of a contemporary site at Linford/Mucking in Essex seems to suggest a large community made up almost exclusively of sunken houses, scattered over a considerable area of Thames gravels. Another site to have received recent attention is Catholme (Staffs) where at the time of writing some sixty-three Saxon timber buildings have been recovered, and these seem to represent the continuous development of seven individual holdings or farmsteads between the sixth and ninth centuries. The subsidiary buildings appear to be in groups, representing individual farmsteads or holdings, all of which were defined by shallow ditches.

There are hints from other sites that not only was the sunken-floored dwelling subsidiary to more regular rectangular buildings, but also that there appears to have been some form of recognizable, if transient, plan to these settlements. A case in point is New Wintles, near Eynsham in Oxfordshire. Here three rectangular post-built structures and ten sunken buildings were found sparsely distributed over an area of 18.6 hectares, together with other structures and possible trackways. The overall plan strongly indicates the presence of larger timber buildings in the spaces. The supposition is that traces of these buildings have been removed by subsequent ploughing. Loom weights and quantities of animal bones again point to a pastoral economy. There are no traces here of a village boundary or a field system as is the case at the nearby Oxfordshire site of Cassington where a similar pattern of dwellings has been identified.

The contrast between these early settlements in layout, building function and building type, and those of the ancestral homelands, is radical, and requires explanation. The excavated settlements may not be typical; orderly plans of farmhouses and ancillary buildings may yet be found. The passage to England may have resulted in drastic changes to the economy but there is another possible explanation. The main sites to have been investigated on the north European coast were all sited on restricted locations, where the ability to spread out was strictly limited and where the need for a well-controlled nucleated community was paramount. It may be that even on the European mainland these highly planned villages were not as typical as has been assumed. In England smaller social groupings, such as pioneering families, could well have encouraged individual or dispersed settlement quite apart from the consequences of a lower population density. New settlement areas may have allowed more space than the rather restricted confines of the settlement mounds at places such as *Feddersen Wierde*; and this may have made close planning unnecessary.

It is quite clear that we are only just beginning to understand the nature of early Saxon settlement. Our ideas are to some extent still tied to old models and it may be that we are searching for patterns of nucleated villages that simply did not exist. Our imprecise dating evidence may also be misleading us about the overall pattern at any one time. It is clear that most early and mid Saxon settlements enjoyed a relatively short life, that settlement mobility within the countryside was the norm and that our medieval village pattern probably comes into being subsequently as a result of land and population pressure.

As we move into the middle and late Saxon periods the picture becomes a little clearer. Settlements were not static during this period either, and there was a great deal of mobility both of buildings and of village plans. At Eaton Socon (Beds), for instance, the plan of the late Saxon village bears little resemblance to the modern one, and the Saxon church is located beneath the castle. It is possible, however, that a lane which runs to the north of the present churchyard perpetuates the line of a pre-Conquest street. Detailed fieldwork on a number of parishes in East Anglia has revealed concentrations of mid Saxon pottery close to isolated churches, and in all the cases examined, the modern village bears little or no resemblance to its Saxon predecessor (Fig. 18).

At Wicken Bonhunt (Essex) recent excavations have revealed dozens of mid Saxon structures of three different phases. These settlements are closely grouped, while an area lying to the east of the structures was open, possibly representing a green for animals. During all phases the settlement was surrounded by a ditch. A similar pattern was found at Maxey (Northants) where continuous occupation of the Roman period was found, and here rectangular buildings of the mid

18. Changes in the village plan at Longham, Norfolk, based on a sixteenth-century plan (top) and fieldwork evidence and map of 1816. These plans graphically illustrate the fluidity of settlement geography over a thousand years. The main phases are (i) middle and late Saxon village based around the church; (ii) migration of the main village to South Hall Green in the early Middle Ages; (iii) migration of village to Kirtling Common in the late Middle Ages; (iv) the enclosure of Kirtling Common leaving a dispersed settlement with two separate linear units (after Wade-Martins 1975).

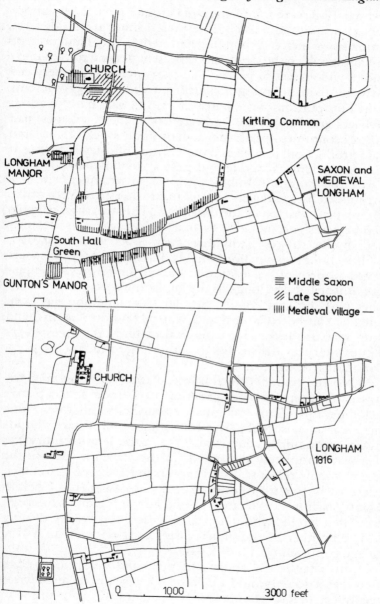

CHURCH

Kirtling Common

LONGHAM
MANOR

SAXON and
MEDIEVAL
LONGHAM

South Hall
Green

GUNTON'S MANOR

≡ Middle Saxon
⁄⁄ Late Saxon
⦀ Medieval village —

CHURCH

LONGHAM
1816

0   1000   3000 feet

Saxon period were found arranged around a relatively empty elongated space. This can be interpreted either as a single farm complex in which each building had an individual function, or a village in which the structures represent peasant tofts and the space a wide street or green. The excavated site lies between the present village and the isolated church but only represents a small proportion of the potential area of Saxon occupation. Archaeological evidence indicates that these villages had mixed economies, partly dependent upon stock raising and grain production, as well as having some industry in the form of iron-working, weaving and pottery manufacture.

At Little Paxton (Cambs), a late Saxon settlement site was surrounded by a gated enclosure. Inside this there were walls, rubbish pits, post-holes and dwellings. The structures covered 86.5 hectares and included formal enclosures. This arrangement might suggest individual farm units with their own ancillary buildings and home-fields. Possibly these farms were served by droveways leading to the village centres. The picture of isolated dwellings in the landscape here is repeated in other parts of East Anglia. Similar fragmentation has been noted at Southoe (Cambs) and Water Newton (Cambs) and quite apart from the archaeological material is suggested by documentary evidence, notably the large number of post-Conquest free tenants.

At North Elmham (Norfolk) excavations have revealed the presence of four periods of pre-Norman Conquest occupation including a pre-Danish compact community. Following this there was an episcopal palace consisting of three major buildings surrounding a courtyard. Late in the tenth century the area was completely replanned. In the eleventh century the area was again replanned, and appears to have been abandoned in the early twelfth century. Further westwards at Chalton (Hants) an impressive range of mid Saxon buildings has been excavated, and it would appear that here too we are dealing with a number of individual farmsteads rather than a true village community (Plate XVI).

In this chapter the terms settlement and village have been used rather loosely, and much of what has been included is negative in that it was intended to dismantle the conventional, easily digestible model of the English settlement. Is there an alternative to explain the creation of the English village? There is a possible hypothesis, which at the moment depends largely upon conjecture. It has been suggested that between the fifth and seventh centuries AD, there was a substantial fall in population (from over two million to under a million?), a trend that was reversed some time after AD 700. It has already been suggested that Romano–British land units survived the end of Roman rule in many areas and that within this framework there was a mixed pattern of transient isolated and nucleated settlement. It has been reasonably argued that the system of cultivation that operated within the Celtic fields was one of infield–outfield, that is, the land nearest the settlement (farmstead or hamlet) was continuously cultivated while that lying at some distance away was only brought into cultivation periodically, thus allowing it to recover its fertility. Over a longer period of time (perhaps fifty to a hundred years), the land nearest to the settlement would become exhausted and there would be a need to move the settlement within the framework of the estate. This system could only operate when there was ample land for cultivation, grazing and semi-permanent fallow.

Given a progressively larger population this system could no longer operate. From about AD 750 onwards, the pressure on land does seem to have increased through a growing population, perhaps caused by a new influx of settlers from Scandinavia. As land pressure increased, even with the introduction of newly cleared ground, the need to regulate agrarian activities became increasingly more important. Against this background we can readily understand the introduction of common or open-field cultivation (two or three field). This system would ensure adequate land for each family, and would also regulate animal grazing on common-land and on the fallow arable between determined dates. Such a system meant that draught animals and ploughs could be kept to a minimum if they were held in common by the community as a whole. The permanent nucleation of the community around a fixed focus such as the church would be a natural development of the process, particularly when the arable was divided into

101

scattered strips throughout the estate. Following on from this would be the ability to control all land resources within the estate – meadow, pasture, common and wood. In the late Saxon period too we see the development of far greater authoritarian control by lord, church and state. The nucleated community was far easier to control than dispersed farmsteads – it can be argued that this was a form of settlement ideally suited to the rigid hierarchy of Norman feudalism.

There are, however, still many unanswered questions concerning the introduction and development of open-field agriculture. Many of the problems of identification of rural settlement are common to the field systems. Archaeological evidence for pre-Conquest open-field agriculture has been located at only two sites, both of these in the rather untypical areas of western Britain: Gwithian (Cornwall) and Hen Domen (Powys). Some historians believe that the adoption of open-field agriculture is a gradual process which culminated only in the thirteenth century. Others point to references to aspects of open-field farming in Saxon documents and argue that it was operating before the Norman Conquest. Whatever the date of its introduction, and we can be sure that there were striking regional differences, open-field agriculture must be seen as the fundamental element in the creation of the nucleated English village.

A pattern is thus emerging of the development of nucleated, but by no means static, communities in eastern and central England during the late Saxon period, say from AD 750 onwards. Some of these villages evolved from, or were the direct descendants of, Roman or pre-Roman communities. The hiatus of rural settlement at the end of the Roman period is now thought of by convention rather than conviction. In the west a far more fragmented settlement pattern was to be found, but even here nucleation was taking place on a smaller scale amidst a background of isolated farms. The late Saxon period also appears to have been one of settlement creation; not only were ancient hamlets developed into nucleated villages, but secondary dependent townships were brought into being with characteristic place-name elements such as *wick*, *cote* and *toft*. Some of these appear to have been based upon isolated farmsteads and it has been suggested on the basis of a case study in Northamptonshire that many of these sites had seen uninterrupted occupation since before the Romans. Others were on new sites and were to form the basis of the colonization of marsh, moor and wood.

By way of a postscript something should be said of the Scandinavian settlement. In England there were two main phases of settlement, the first between 850 and 866 when, in spite of the successful local resistance of Wessex under Alfred, the Danes seized and settled in the eastern part of Mercia, all East Anglia and all but the northern parts of Northumberland; the second when an invasion composed largely of Norwegians settled to the west of the Pennines. Despite the intensity of the settlement little archaeological evidence has been located, and almost all the settlement sites which have been investigated are in Scotland. It is therefore difficult to say anything about the nature of Scandinavian rural settlement apart from observations based on place-name evidence. It is generally agreed that the suffix *-by* is indicative of primary Scandinavian settlement, although *-by* endings are often attached to already existing Anglo-Saxon settlements. In some cases a Scandinavian personal name prefix is followed by an Anglian suffix – for example Branston, Flixton, Sproxton and Thurgarton. In east Yorkshire, for instance, over seventy hybrid names of Anglian origin have been identified. Some minor names incorporating the elements *holme* and *carr* appear to indicate Danish colonization of marshy land. It therefore seems probable that many so-called Scandinavian villages were already in existence when the settlers arrived. It is possible that the Scandinavian incursions provided a catalyst which stimulated the creation of nucleated villages in northern Britain. But we can no longer accept the simple explanation that different settlement patterns were the creation of different ethnic groups. There are many questions remaining about Scandinavian settlement, such as the relative paucity of Scandinavian place-names in East Anglia, but the answer to this, along with the others, must await further archaeological discovery.

SELECT BIBLIOGRAPHY

Chisholm, M., *Rural Settlement and Land Use* (2nd revised ed., 1968).

Finberg, H. P. R. (ed.), *The Agrarian History of England and Wales*, Vol. I, II (1972).

Gelling, M., *Signposts to the Past* (1978).

Hoskins, W. G., *The Making of the English Landscape* (1955).

Jones, G., 'Settlement Patterns in Anglo-Saxon England', *Antiquity*, 35 (1961).

Leeds, E. T., *The Archaeology of the Anglo-Saxon Settlements* (1913).

Taylor, C., *Fields in the English Landscape* (1975).

Wilson, D. M. (ed.), *The Archaeology of Anglo-Saxon England* (1976).

5　The medieval village

The Norman Conquest provides a convenient divide for the examination of English history. It marks the welding together of the Anglo-Saxon and Scandinavian states and the establishment of a single, if disturbed, English kingdom. It also marks a watershed in our knowledge of the land and its inhabitants, because it was at this point that the Domesday Book of 1086 was compiled, ostensibly providing us with detailed information about settlement and agriculture in the eleventh century. The changes associated with the Norman Conquest were often more political than economic or social, although it is certainly true that in the north and west military reparations following uprisings resulted in the widespread obliteration of many settlements, and their re-establishment a generation later. Nevertheless, the accession of King William to the throne and the beginning of feudal England does tend to foster the illusion that we know more of rural settlement at this time than we really do. This illusion is enhanced by the first reference to the vast majority of our villages in the Domesday Book, but the study of early medieval villages has as many pitfalls as that of any other period. To begin with there is a dangerous gap of documentation between the late eleventh century and the emergence of good consistent manorial records in the thirteenth century. It is all too easy to transfer concepts of the village of 1300 back eight generations to the time of the Norman Conquest.

If we accept that all ages are periods of transition, we must now see the Domesday Survey of 1086 as recording a stage in an evolving landscape – not, as has been conventionally thought, surveying the culmination of the Saxon settlement.

Although most of our current village names are to be found for the first time within the folios of Domesday, many are not and we can no longer be certain at all times what these names are referring to – a farmstead, a hamlet or even a group of villages. The Domesday Book appears to incorporate a high degree of artificiality in its assessment figures. It is not concerned with individual units of settlement, but with taxable estates. Hence everywhere there are blanket assessments that can deceive us about the true nature of the settlement pattern. In Shropshire, for instance, in addition to some 440 named places, a further 191 'berewicks' are mentioned, each of these representing a dependent village or hamlet. In other manors dependent settlements are not even mentioned as such, but are included within an overall assessment. Stoke St Milborough was assessed at twenty hides (units of five hides commonly being used emphasizing the artificial nature of Domesday figures); later records show that this covered five other settlements within the manor. Even manors assessed at only a modest hideage could conceal a large number of dependent townships. It has been suggested that some of these large multiple estates were of considerable antiquity, possibly dating back to the Roman period or earlier. The Norman Conquest virtually obliterated this ancient estate system in many parts of England by a process of fragmentation.

Nevertheless, despite its many drawbacks, the Domesday Book does provide us with some sort of a picture of eleventh-century England. It was already a densely populated country. The population was not, however, uniformly distributed, the highest population being in East Anglia and gradually thinning out towards the west. By 1086 almost all the potentially good agricultural land was under cultivation, although there were still some notably blank areas, such as the forest lands of north Warwickshire, which were colonized during the following two centuries, and the dry sandy soil belt of Surrey, Berkshire and Hampshire. These were not brought into cultivation until the seventeenth and eighteenth centuries. Generally speaking there were not the large expanses of 'wilderness' available for systematic colonization found in continental Europe at this time. All that remained for the increasing population of the early Middle Ages to colonize was land which was essentially marginal. The developments of the early Middle Ages should therefore be seen against a background of dwindling land resources.

In Domesday we are seeing a countryside in the process of filling up, a process that was to continue for a further two centuries, and by 1300 it is estimated that the level of population could have been as high as five million. The precise effects of this growth on the settlement pattern are difficult to gauge, but by 1300, when we have a reasonably complete archaeological and daunting body of documentary records, the pattern is fairly clear. In some places these enable all aspects of village life to be reconstructed – seigneurial and ecclesiastic administration, the economic and social life, and occasionally even the detailed evolution of the village morphology.

By 1300 settlement nucleation was to be found over much of the country. Compact and often well-regulated villages with dependent villas or townships all sitting within their own open fields distributed at roughly one-and-a-half kilometre intervals were normal over much of lowland England. Naturally the details varied considerably from village to village and from one area to another, but in general terms each village had its church, manor house and more humble tenements sited close to each other, and were surrounded by a considerable acreage of arable land, normally divided up into strips. A mass of tracks and ways serviced the fields and eventually led to common meadows, pasture, waste and woodland. The lord would have reserved a certain area of 'demesne' or land for his own cultivation. Where seigneurial control was strong, as it was in many parts of the kingdom, the lord would reserve certain areas for his exclusive activities such as hunting.

The large nucleated village was of course not universal. Many dependent townships occupying the less attractive land were by their very nature often quite small, and in areas where pastoral farming continued to dominate, the need for regulation was less and the dispersed hamlet and isolated farm continued in being. In medieval Wales, for instance, the ideal bond hamlet was legally thought to contain only nine houses. Here the infield–outfield system persisted, with grazing on the extensive common pastures, parts of which were subject to temporary cultivation.

Whatever the detailed arrangements, however, the picture that emerges is of a tightly managed landscape. The manorial court was responsible for the regulation of internal field boundaries, the precise amount of grazing and rights of gathering on the common waste, and it also looked after the trackways and the streams. The manor court also collectively administered rules of husbandry, watched over local customs of tenure and inheritance and enforced local peace and order. By 1300 may be seen a landscape which was being intensively used at a subsistence level. A glance at an aerial photograph (Plate XVII) will show just how intensive that cultivation was, with terracing introduced in some areas to exploit even the valley slopes which had not previously been cultivated. Traces of medieval field cultivation in the form of ridge and furrow are to be found at heights of over 300 metres on moorland and hillside. Professor Postan concludes:

> In the older parts of England the lands taken up for the first time by the arable farmers in the thirteenth century were as a rule of the lowest possible quality; too forbidding to have tempted the settlers of earlier centuries, and some of them too unremunerative to have been maintained in cultivation by farmers of a later age.

The countryside was already too full to enable the plantation of a rash of new villages; the equivalent of the French *villeneuve* were the new urban centres which sprang up throughout the countryside in the twelfth and thirteenth centuries and absorbed some of the surplus rural population. Some new towns such as Alnmouth (Northumb) and New Romney (Kent) were laid out completely afresh and despite modest success never developed beyond the size of a large village. Others such as Baschurch and Ruyton-XI-Towns (Salop) were grafted onto existing villages and failed, although vestiges of their original design can be detected in the modern village plans.

At a more modest level there is ample evidence to show that many hamlets were being created or expanded in the twelfth

108

and thirteenth centuries. These were often based on isolated farms or in the case of Lychett Minster (Dorset), field chapels; here the chapel lay on the edge of Wareham Forest and was first recorded in 1244, when marginal land was being developed. The records of 'assarting' (land colonization) everywhere tell a story of land, often of a very inferior quality, being brought into cultivation.

There were a few areas where more ambitious village colonization took place. Certain large-scale drainage enterprises in the fens created completely new villages during the early Middle Ages. Fleet (Lincs) was one of these, and was composed of a regular row of homesteads sited next to their portions of the newly reclaimed fields, each of which stretched into the fen. Today many fenland 'villages' have been all but abandoned in favour of the less-exposed settlements on the fen edge.

Thus it would appear that the permanent nucleated village so familiar to us today was a factor not of ethnic or cultural change, but of economic and social forces. It was brought about by a complex combination of increasing population and increasing authoritarian control through the manorial system. The need to maximize food production was matched by increased control by the owners of land, and, as it happened, the church also tightened its control at the same time. Many communities which previously had possessed dependent chapels or had been served from a central minster-church, gained their own church in the twelfth century, thus becoming the centre for the parish which was often coextensive with the manor. The creation of new churches and parishes, which was a feature of the late Saxon and early Norman period reinforced the emphasis on a nodal settlement. The very presence of a large, imposing stone building in the village had a stabilizing effect upon the geography of the settlement and psychology of the community.

The overall rigidity of land tenure that had developed appears virtually to have brought about an end to settlement mobility for a short while. Of course a settlement pattern can never be absolutely static and there are numerous examples of changes during the thirteenth and fourteenth centuries.

109

Nevertheless, the basic pattern of village distribution was established and fossilized by 1300, the constraints imposed by a strictly disciplined communal agrarian system being such that it required the very erosion of that system to enable settlement mobility to operate once more on a large scale.

One of the problems involved in writing about a national phenomenon such as the village is that local and regional differences are so marked that generalization is often invalid. Nevertheless if we are right in linking open-field agriculture with village nucleation, it can now be demonstrated as a widespread agrarian feature of the Middle Ages. Writers such as H. L. Gray in his book *English Field Systems* (1915) limited the distribution of open-field arable primarily to the Midlands. Later scholars using a wide variety of sources, however, have come to the conclusion that open-field agriculture was to be found in every English county, and even in the lowland areas of central and southern Wales. Even in central and western Wales open-field strip farming was introduced when circumstances were favourable, and in the south-west, areas such as north-western Somerset and Devon indicate evidence of open-field agriculture in the lower, flatter, more fertile coastal plains. This requires a rejection of the traditional concept of open-field agriculture being a feature of the Anglo-Saxon settlement, which it quite clearly was not. Gray's map of the Midland field system more accurately represents the areas of open-field survival into the post-medieval period, than its original distribution. The most commonly cited case of open-field farming is that at Laxton (Northants), where a form of common agriculture survives today (Fig. 19). We can perhaps take the argument a little further; in the south-west, the Welsh border and the north-west there appears to have been an uneven move towards open-field farming and settlement nucleation in the early Middle Ages. Often land (sometimes lying at well over 300 metres) which in the long run was totally unsuitable for arable was brought into cultivation, although one must always remember that there were considerable local variations in the practice of open-field husbandry. As soon as local pressure for land was eased, the land reverted to its traditional use as pasture. The main reason for this would

110

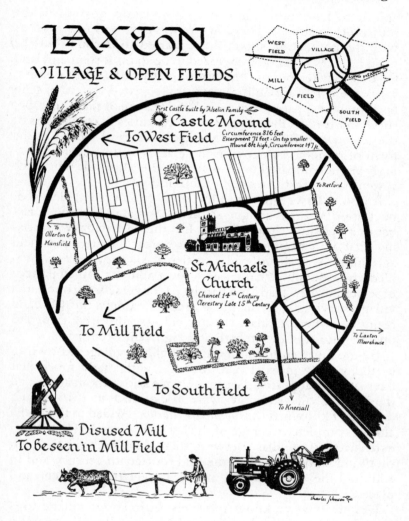

19. Diagrammatic representation of the open-field system at Laxton, Northamptonshire, where a form of open field agriculture is still practised. It is ironic that Laxton, which is the most commonly quoted example of a typical medieval village, appears originally to have lain on a different axis running northwards from the church to the castle and was probably re-planned in its present form in the early Middle Ages.

111

appear to have been the end of population growth in the fourteenth century. There are numerous complex reasons why the population should have started to decline, but the main result was that arable ceased to be so important and land fell or was taken out of cultivation and turned over to pasture. Thus open-field agriculture with its associated system of strip farming was apparently a short-lived feature of the landscape, surviving for less than two or three centuries in some parts of the country. It follows that the archaeological record in the form of ridge-and-furrow in these areas will be correspondingly slight compared to areas such as the Midlands where the system survived for nearly a thousand years.

It also follows that once the open-field system decayed, nucleation was no longer so necessary and in some cases became a positive disadvantage. It is therefore hardly surprising that it was precisely in those areas where open-field agriculture was abandoned first that the village fabric crumbled earliest of all. We then see a reversion to a mixed pattern of scattered farmsteads and hamlets. Conversely the nucleated village survived best in those areas – namely the Midland counties – where regulated open-field agriculture continued to operate into the seventeenth and eighteenth centuries.

By the fourteenth century almost all the villages known to us today were in existence, together with many more that have since disappeared. Fortunately we know about almost all the English villages which were in existence in 1316 from a document known as the *Nomina Villarum*. Added to this is the almost complete coverage of the lay subsidy of 1334, with its extensive lists of villas. Between them there are over fourteen thousand named places in the mid fourteenth century and in addition the rolls include many unspecified hamlets and places.

Despite this we know relatively little about village topography or about the dwellings within the villages. Generally speaking medieval documents are silent about the shape and form of the settlements they are recording. A few rare surveys include topographical information, such as the rentals of the Peterborough Abbey manors (*c.* 1400) which describe the tenants' houses as they lay along the village streets. More

112

common are indirect references, such as those included in a mid fourteenth-century rental for Sherborne (Glos) which located the tenements in the 'East End' and 'West End' of the village. The division between the two ends survives today, the church and manor lying at either extreme. Later layouts have replaced the medieval ones, and newer houses have obliterated traces of their predecessors. Even the shape of a village in the fifteenth or sixteenth century may be no guide to its plan two or three centuries earlier. If we compare the plans of the village of Boarstall (Bucks) as it appears on one of the very earliest maps dated 1444 with the settlement as it appears today we can see that there is very little correlation between the two. The excavations of many deserted medieval village sites have warned us of the dangers of taking later village plans too literally; many sites seem to have been laid out anew in the thirteenth or fourteenth centuries. We must be wary of discussing medieval villages in terms of the present form or from their form as seen on the first maps. In much the same way as many place-names have changed beyond recognition, so too have the villages to which they are attached.

The only village buildings of the fourteenth century which survive today are those which were built of stone, namely churches, manor houses and occasional barns. While the churches survive in considerable numbers, there are comparatively few medieval manor houses. There are, however, enough to show that the manor houses of the early fourteenth century were either of the simple, rectangular, first-floor hall type dating from the twelfth to the thirteenth centuries, or of the newer end-hall types. In all manor houses the emphasis was on the hall, the home of the lord and the place of the manorial court, where accounts were audited and records kept. As the nearest equivalent to a public building it usually warranted the use of stone. The moated manorial homestead was in fashion at this time and was especially characteristic of late colonized woodland areas such as Essex, Suffolk and the Arden of Warwickshire where land had been sub-let to new freeholders. Many moated manor houses were sited outside the village, although some were inserted within the framework of the community (see Fig. 7). In contrast, while many of the peasant houses had stone wall footings, they were, generally speaking, much more flimsy structures and none have survived intact. What appears to be certain is that they were regularly renovated or completely rebuilt.

Industrial villages of the Middle Ages

Industrial activity was never completely absent from village life, but some settlements depended heavily on local industry. Archaeology is beginning to demonstrate that industry was a feature of some late Saxon villages although it is not until the Middle Ages that we have substantial documentary evidence. The Domesday Book hints at the existence of specialist industrial activity, with references to mining and lead working at Ashford, Bakewell, Crich and Winksworth (Derby); salt pans are recorded in every seaboard county from Lincolnshire to Cornwall; at Ollerton (Devon) thirty-three saltworkers were recorded and twenty-seven at Lyme (Dorset), while later documents show that there was extensive industrial activity in the Weald of Kent and the Forest of Dean. During the Middle Ages, however, industry was rarely disassociated from its agricultural base, with the result that most industry was contained within existing settlements. For instance, the pottery workers of Lyveden (Northants) were occupying the normal agrarian holdings within the village, and were almost certainly continuing to cultivate their land simultaneously. A similar pattern seems to have operated at Brill (Bucks) where the kilns for the famous potteries were worked in backyard areas. In the West Riding of Yorkshire cloth workers were also agricultural workers. Barnack (Lincs) was one of the best-known sources of building stone anywhere in England during the Middle Ages, yet despite the surrounding pock-marked landscape, the medieval village of Barnack was no larger than its neighbours, and its present form tells little of this activity. In these cases industry had little direct impact on the physical character of the village.

The woollen industry which developed in the Pennines, Cotswolds, East Anglia and the south-east during the late Middle Ages was rather different. By the fifteenth century up to half of the working population in some parts of the country, was involved in cloth production. These industries were essentially rural and led to the expansion of old centres and the creation of new ones. They are also important because they were growing at a time when many rural settlements based purely on agriculture were declining. In Wiltshire, for instance, dyers, fullers and weavers were drawn out of the towns to the sites of the new mills in the valleys around Salisbury. Eventually, however, the Wiltshire clothiers shifted their attention to the north-west of the county between Malmesbury and Westbury, and to the south-east around Mere. In these areas of pastoral dairying, where the owners of smallholdings had time to combine dairying with another occupation, the Wiltshire cloth industry subsequently made its home.

The early woollen industry did not, however, automatically affect the form or outward appearance of the village. Early industry was largely part time and the community almost always maintained a strong agricultural element. The cloth-working villages of the Cotswolds and Suffolk however, housed large numbers of independent weavers in the late Middle Ages and accordingly contained a considerable proportion of smallholdings and cottages; this often resulted in a less regular arrangement than in the wholly agrarian community. This was in marked contrast to later industrial settlements which were often consciously designed to meet a particular need. Often the only obvious sign would have been in the form of buildings adapted for industrial use, the spinning gallery or insertion of large attic windows to give light. Often it is the public buildings, the parish church or the market hall, which provide the best manifestation of local industrial activity.

Nevertheless, as the scale of industrial activity increased, as its technology and financing changed, so too did its effect on the pattern of rural settlement. During the later Middle Ages it was the cloth industry which above all generated wealth. In many cases the houses and public buildings reflect this prosperity as well as the churches. Lavenham (Suffolk) is the classic example, but there are numerous others in the Cotswolds in

115

the south-west and even in the Pennines, although here much of the evidence has been swept away or consumed by the overwhelming impact of later industries.

Lavenham has a composite village plan, dominated by the parish church, which started from a square and grew outwards as a result of medieval prosperity (Fig. 20). This wealth of the late fifteenth and early sixteenth century came to East Anglia at a time when church building satisfied both private piety and public ostentation. It also led to a virtual rebuilding of the medieval village in a single architectural style, with the result that the tradesmen's shops, the cloth halls, the inns, the houses of the merchant clothiers and even the weavers' cottages still reflect a distant prosperity. Lavenham's fame was short lived as the locally made blue broadcloth was replaced by the New Draperies manufactured elsewhere; the village reverted largely to agriculture and was therefore saved from the rebuilding and reconstruction that came to other longer-lived clothing towns such as Sudbury and Hadleigh.

The pattern of the new industrial settlements was highly individualistic and markedly different from that of the old. It was not confined within the walls or even the suburbs of the old town, and was often a straggling growth integrated only by its market place and by the parish church, itself wholly or partly rebuilt at this time. Kersey and Long Melford, two other clothmaking centres in Suffolk, still exhibit linear patterns of regulated growth along a main street. The expansion of industries in the countryside is still exemplified at Castle Combe in Wiltshire, where during the first half of the fifteenth century there was an impressive industrial growth along the stream with the building of new, and rebuilding of old, houses, many of them in local stone. Among these new buildings at Castle Combe was a fifteenth-century church tower with decorations based on cloth working implements. Here a growing class of craftsmen with no agricultural holdings lived in the valleys at Nethercombe, while yeoman cultivators lived on the heights above the wooded valley at Overcombe. Even in the old part of the town this pressure was felt and, at a time when many rural settlements were declining in the mid

116

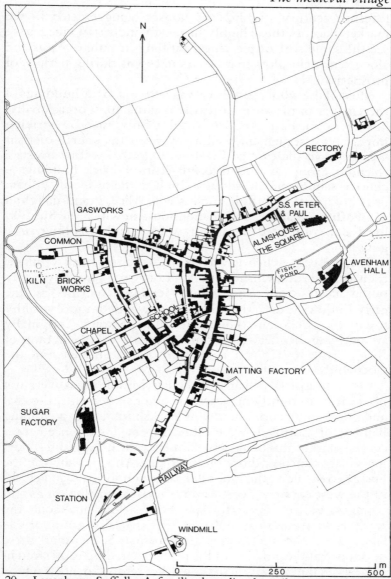

N

RECTORY

GASWORKS

COMMON

S.S. PETER
& PAUL

ALMSHOUSE
THE SQUARE

FISH-
POND

LAVENHAM
HALL

KILN BRICK-
WORKS

SCHOOL

CHAPEL

MATTING FACTORY

SUGAR
FACTORY

RAILWAY

STATION

WINDMILL

0   250   500 m

20. Lavenham, Suffolk. A fossilized medieval textile town, which has retained a number of village features. In the nineteenth century it had some elements of urban life, such as the gasworks and some small factories.

117

fifteenth century, we hear of houses being erected in the market place. In those highly successful industrial villages we see the same sort of piecemeal infilling in public places and along tenement plots that occurs in towns during periods of prosperity.

Most of the wool prosperity was reflected in the buildings of the villages in the areas of textile manufacture; occasionally, however, an East Anglian wool family made a striking impact on a settlement well away from the source of their wealth, as in the case of Ewelme (Oxon). Ewelme boasts a splendid group of mid fifteenth-century brick buildings – church, school and almshouses, built to the order of William de la Pole, Earl of Suffolk and his wife Alice, grand-daughter of Geoffrey Chaucer. The manor house in which the Suffolks lived and completed the picturesque assembly is long since gone.

This process, when it was expressed at its most virulent, transformed rural villages into major towns. Thus Lavenham raised itself from an obscure country village in the early Middle Ages to the rank of the twentieth most wealthy town by 1525. In Gloucestershire, Stroud, originally an outlying hamlet dependent chapelry of the manor of Bisley, rose to a position of industrial prominence in the Cotswolds.

Other industrial villages of the late Middle Ages were not necessarily so tightly nucleated as other settlements; the coal and iron mining communities of Yorkshire and the tin mining hamlets of Cornwall were often dispersed – the need for a central market area being less. Similarly the fishing and seafaring villages such as those on the Battle Abbey estates on the Sussex coast, along the Norfolk coast or on the bays and creeks of the west country, were assemblages of smallholdings and cottages, which appear to have been strung out along the seashore or around bays. Yet another specialist group of villages were the mercantile settlements. Sometimes these developed at the junction of the principal trading routes and in some cases they simply acted as market centres for areas which had no town nearby – often carrying the place-name prefix 'Chipping' or 'Market' (Plate XVIII).

118

The deserted medieval village

The closest we can really come to most medieval villages is through the investigation of deserted villages. Since the creation of the Deserted Medieval Village Research Group (now the Medieval Village Research Group) in 1952, considerable attention has been paid to abandoned medieval settlements in this country. Whereas twenty-five years ago only a handful of such sites had been identified, we now know that there are over two-and-a-half thousand deserted villages in England alone, and as work progresses each year new sites are located. Some 220 sites have been identified in Lincolnshire, 165 in Northumberland and over 400 in Yorkshire. Even in those parts of the country, such as the south-west and north-east, where such villages were initially not recognized, they are to be found in abundance; although quite insignificant totals of abandoned villages are recorded for counties such as Herefordshire and Cumberland, there is no doubt that this reflects the lack of detailed fieldwork rather than the absence of such features. In Shropshire, for instance, only a handful of sites was known when a national distribution map was drawn up in 1966; since then well over a hundred sites have been located, and the picture is still far from complete. The subject has been reviewed in a book of major importance edited by Maurice Beresford and John Hurst, entitled, *Deserted Medieval Villages* (1971). This deals in detail with the development of the study of abandoned medieval settlements from both the historical and archaeological viewpoint, and provides a wealth of information concerning medieval occupation.

Before we move on to the examination of the physical remains from deserted villages some attention should be paid to the causes of village abandonment during the Middle Ages. Few settlement desertions can be attributed to the twelfth and thirteenth centuries as this was generally speaking a period of village expansion. In Leicestershire, for instance, only four villages disappeared between 1086 and the early fourteenth-century tax assessments, and these desertions were almost certainly the result of the operation of Cistercian abbeys whose rule prescribed solitude and whose farming could be

119

continued away from village centres. This pattern is to be found across the country; there are some places where changes in the physical geography actually caused the loss of villages. On the east coast of Yorkshire, a strip of land up to one-and-a-half kilometres wide in the area of Holderness was removed by coastal erosion in the thirteenth century, with the result that an estimated twenty villages simply disappeared.

The most common scapegoat chosen as the cause of village abandonment is the 'Black Death' of 1348–9, and while it is true that both the rural and urban populations suffered severely there is little contemporary documentation to vindicate this argument. Too many villages throughout the country as a whole were paying substantial contributions to poll taxes collected during the second half of the fourteenth century to suggest the mass destruction of rural settlements. It is true that there are one or two instances where the Black Death was clearly responsible for instant depopulation. At Hale in Apeforth parish (Northants), for example, in 1356 we hear 'the premises are worth nothing now because no one dwells or has dwelt in Hale since the pestilence', and this is confirmed later in the century when it was recorded that Hale was still worth nothing 'because the messuages are wasted'. The marginal siting of this township probably made it more vulnerable to permanent devastation than larger villages. At Tusmore in Oxfordshire the lord transformed the empty holdings into a deer park, and at Bolton near Bradford (N. Yorks) the tax collectors of 1379 found 'not a sole remaining'. It is true that many other villages were smaller in the latter part of the fourteenth century as a result of the plague, during which their fabric had been dealt a severe blow, but most of them continued with an increased area of pasture and a decline in arable.

It would appear that the growth in the number of people before 1300 had been such that it had overstretched the resources of the land to support the inflated population. All over Europe natural disasters such as poor harvests, soil exhaustion and pestilence took their toll during the fourteenth century, a decline that was not to be arrested until the sixteenth century, and in some rural areas not until the mid eighteenth century was there any marked reversal of this trend. The Black Death, devastating though it was, simply contributed to an already deteriorating situation. In the Cambridge area, for instance, it is estimated that the population was nearly halved between the late thirteenth and early sixteenth centuries. The population had been so dense in East Anglia that the effects of the decline were particularly spectacular. The depopulation of the Norfolk countryside can be measured through the number of ruined churches. Of about 900 medieval churches, well over a quarter have been abandoned, while nearly 250 are in ruins.

The decline in population naturally had its effects on settlements, and between 1300 and 1600 there is a steady process of settlement decay and abandonment; this was a relatively gradual process up until the mid fifteenth century. From 1450 onwards there was a massive change in land use from arable to grass. The form of agriculture which required a substantial number of husbandmen in the village changed to a pastoral form with a much smaller labour force. The stimulus to this change in land use came from a massive and continuing expansion of the demand for wool coupled with the fall in population. Some authorities believe that the earlier stages of this demand had been met by using the post-plague surplus arable land for grazing and that the continuing pressure for wool had been met in part by overstocking the commons with sheep, but the full impact could only be met by landlords and tenants deciding to make the complete transition from arable to pastoral husbandry.

The late medieval swing from corn to grass involved the total area of a township's fields and was an almost irreversible action resulting in the end of arable husbandry. Agricultural workers were superfluous and their houses simply fell into decay. Without villagers there was no village. From the late thirteenth to the late eighteenth centuries there was little incentive to change back to cereal production and when corn was eventually sown again over the sheep pastures there was no return of the natives to the village. A new arable landscape was managed from a small number of farmsteads located conveniently throughout the township, and there was no need for villagers to return with their ploughs.

121

Thus the changing demographic and economic pattern of the late Middle Ages brought about the elimination of nearly one-quarter of the village settlements of medieval England, and seriously weakened the structure of many more. The reasons why some villages were lost and others survived is still a matter of some controversy. Obviously a proportion of those abandoned were marginal; those settlements that had been pushed towards and beyond the margin of cultivation were naturally vulnerable and many of them succumbed. Those that occupied difficult or unpleasant sites were also obvious candidates for destruction. There were, however, many others in Midland England that appear to have suffered because of the opportunism of the local lord rather than any inherent weakness in their ability to survive. Whole groups of villages on the Warwickshire/Oxfordshire border were wiped off the map by enterprising lords taking advantage of high wool prices, leaving a landscape unnaturally empty of nucleated settlements. It is an interesting exercise to examine a modern 1 : 50,000 map and see the substantial gap where villages obviously once stood, and guess the reasons for the continued existence of the survivors – a busy road, a bridge or even an unworldly lord, who failed to see the financial advantages of conversion from arable to pasture (Fig. 21).

Hundreds of sites have received some attention over the past twenty years but, because of the nature of the archaeological record, the progress of excavation is slow. Unlike urban sites, deeply stratified deposits do not normally develop under rural conditions, so considerable care has to be taken in the process of excavation. It appears that during the late twelfth and thirteenth centuries, over much of the country where stone is to be found there was a change from constructing peasant houses in wood and turf to stone. This trend appears to start in the south and south-west and then move northwards. The change may possibly be accounted for by the diminution of timber through the clearing of woodland for agriculture, although it is quite clear that coppice-land was managed to provide a regular wood supply throughout the Middle Ages. The stone used was normally available locally, but occasion-

122

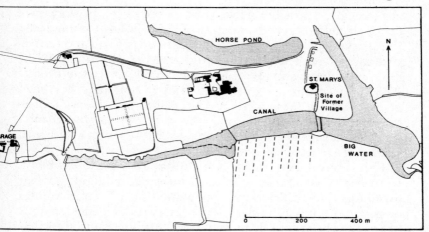

21. Fawsley, Northamptonshire. Typical Midland deserted village – all
that survives from the emparking by the Knightly family in the early
sixteenth century is the church and the great house. To the west of the house
there lies an area of formal gardens.

ally more exotic stone, reused from a manor house or church
has been found. Only buildings of this nature will have had
well-cut stone and sometimes mouldings; similarly they
would have been the only buildings using mortar, although
clay bonding was fairly common. In some areas where stone is
not readily accessible there may have been intensive stone
robbing.

Another feature to emerge from recent excavation is the fact
that vernacular building traditions are of some antiquity. For
example, in the chalklands of Yorkshire and Lincolnshire the
buildings were always of chalk, not flint, while in the southern
chalk areas the buildings were mainly of flint. It is believed that
in parts of the country during the later Middle Ages some
buildings were constructed of timber sitting on low stone sill.
It is not quite clear what initiated this change, but it may be
related to the greater availability of timber due to the
economic decline of the fourteenth and fifteenth centuries.

In the clay areas to the south-east and north-west of the
stone belt the change from timber to stone construction would

123

not have been possible. Fieldwork on these sites provide evidence of flat tofts with no sign of solid house foundations. Excavation has demonstrated the existence of cob and timber structures which leave very little trace apart from soils of different colours and textures. For example, at Barton Blount (Derby) a complex sequence of timber buildings has been uncovered, but these were never replaced by stone or stone-based structures. On the other hand at Faxton (Northants) crude stone sills were introduced, probably from a source of stone not far away.

The survival of evidence is such that it is often possible to recover a considerable amount of information about peasant dwellings (Fig. 22). Floors were either of clay, stone cobbles or covered with stone flags; on a few sites evidence of floor boards has been found. In many peasant houses no floor has survived, mainly as a result of constant clearing, which, quite apart from removing any floor, also means that stratified deposits have been removed. Most roofs were constructed of perishable material such as turf, reeds or straw, and, in consequence, very little evidence for roofing has survived. The key cause of constant rebuilding of houses during the medieval period may well have been the poor roofing, which enabled dampness to penetrate the walls, and thus necessitated rebuilding every generation or so.

On those sites where there has been extensive excavation it has proved possible to trace the development or decline of houses, enclosures and outbuildings over a considerable period of time. At Upton (Glos), for instance, one dwelling started as a long-house with animals and humans sharing the same roof and entrance. To this was added a barn extension entered through a separate door, and finally a completely separate outbuilding for animals was constructed, giving the basis of the later farm, farmyard and subsidiary farm buildings. A similar pattern of farmhouse development was traced at Gomeldon (Wilts). At Wharram Percy (N. Yorks), where the most extensive excavations on any deserted village site in Britain have taken place, numerous dwellings were built on top of another, indicating a rebuilding approximately every thirty years. Elsewhere too this pattern of continuity and

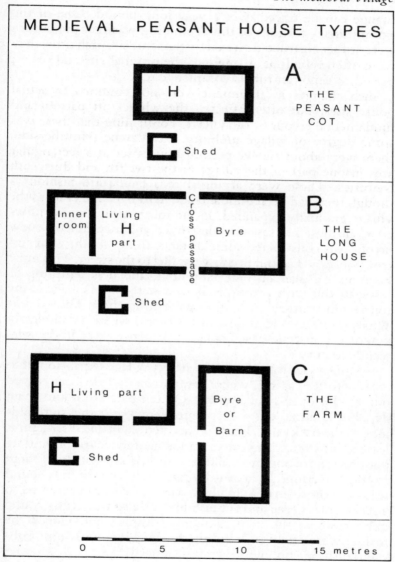

22. Medieval peasant house types commonly found on deserted village sites (after Beresford and Hurst 1971).

change can be traced over a very long period. One of the extraordinary features of this rebuilding was that the houses were not reconstructed on exactly the same site each time; they were often rebuilt at an angle to the original site and over a period of time can turn a complete circle.

Such changes in alignment were not confined to actual house sites, but often affected the whole toft pattern and fundamental layout of the village, confirming that there was some degree of village mobility. At Wawne (Humberside) there were about twelve peasant houses set in a rectangular area in one part of the village in the twelfth and thirteenth centuries. These were arranged in a haphazard fashion as though they had been built and added to over the years as the village gradually expanded. In the fourteenth century, however, all these houses were destroyed and a completely new layout was constructed some distance to the south, with sixteen houses all laid out in a row parallel to the street. This must have been a planned redevelopment, and it is tempting to associate this with a completely new start to the village in the fourteenth century. A similar pattern has been observed at Wharram Percy and at Seacourt (Oxon), where a completely new street of stone-based houses was constructed in the thirteenth century.

In some cases it is possible to detect village expansion onto areas of former arable, where new tenements have been carved out of the open-field system. Quite apart from the main dwellings, barns, and byres, there were often other outbuildings in the backyard. These were often short-lived structures leaving little trace, and as excavation has tended to concentrate upon the more obvious buildings, little is known about them from excavation. The corn-drying kiln is a commonly found feature in the form of a circular oven with a long flue leading to a stoke hole. Oven and rubbish pits are also frequently found quite close to the main building complex and indeed the former were rarely built within the dwelling house until substantial stone chimneys were introduced.

SELECT BIBLIOGRAPHY

Allison, K. J., *Deserted Villages* (1970).
Baker, A. R. H. and Harley, J. B. (eds), *Man Made the Land* (1973).
Baker, A. R. H. and Butlin, R. A. (eds), *Studies of Field Systems in the British Isles* (1973).
Beresford, M. W. and St Joseph, J. K. S., *Medieval England, an Aerial Survey* (1958).
Beresford, M. W. and Hurst, J. G. (eds), *Deserted Medieval Villages* (1971).
Hilton, R. H., *A Medieval Society* (1966).
Postan, M. M., *The Medieval Economy and Society* (1972).
Sawyer, P. H. (ed.), *Medieval Settlement* (1976).

6   The changing village 1600–1900

Conventionally the Middle Ages are thought of as the heyday of village England and until quite recently relatively little attention has been paid to the study of rural settlement after 1600. The development of towns, commerce and above all the Industrial Revolution have emphasized the importance of the process of urbanization in the period between 1600 and 1900. Nevertheless, the population of Britain remained predominantly rural until the middle decades of the nineteenth century, and for most people the village remained home until that date. In 1801 only 19 per cent of the population lived in towns with over 20,000 inhabitants and as late as 1851 agriculture remained the largest single source of employment in Britain. Even after the great exodus to the towns which occurred in the late nineteenth century, villages remained an important element in the economic and social life of the nation.

Over central England the most dramatic changes were associated with the agrarian revolution. The process of eliminating communal open-field farming, which had already been achieved in the west, continued relentlessly, until by the middle of the nineteenth century open-field strips were a rarity anywhere in Britain. In some Midland counties well over half the land was taken out of open-field cultivation and enclosed in regular fields between 1600 and 1800. The effect on many settlements was devastating. Parliamentary enclosure involved the rapid creation of a new pattern of farm holdings that were frequently sited at some distance from the old centre of settlement. Eventually this resulted in the extensive rebuilding of farmhouses outside the villages and a consequent weakening of the village structure, particularly where enclos-

XIII March. Romano–British earthwork.

XIV Creek Fen.

XV Cropmark traces of probable mid Saxon buildings at Drayton, Oxfordshire. The rectangular structures appear to represent buildings lying around a large central open area. They are part of a complex which includes an early Saxon settlement site.

XVI The post-hole traces of rectangular buildings of a mid Saxon settlement site at Chalton, Hampshire.

XVII The intensity of medieval land use is clearly demonstrated by this
aerial view of ridge and furrow from the former open fields of Southam,
Warwickshire. The open fields were enclosed at the time of Parliamentary
enclosure and were cut by the Oxford Canal which runs across the centre of
the photograph. In the background is the scattered village of Napton on the
Hill and a secondary settlement called Chapel Green.

XVIII   Chittlehampton, Devon. A tightly knit village based on a central market square with recent development on the roads leading into the village. In an area where nucleated settlements are rare this village served as a market centre for a large region on the edge of Exmoor. The church is dedicated to St Urith, a local saint martyred in the sixth century, indicating an early foundation. Its remarkable west tower suggests commercial prosperity at the end of the Middle Ages.

XIX   A decaying rural settlement pattern in Shropshire. The dispersed cottages were constructed for the lead industry during the eighteenth and nineteenth cenuries in a haphazard manner on the edge of moorland.

ure was achieved quickly. The removal of the farmhouse resulted in farmworkers' cottages falling into decay as they were either rehoused in the farm or in new cottages built away from the village. Thus the original 'raison d'être' of the village in the form of an association of farmsteads was removed, although of course many farms did continue to operate from a village base well into this century.

In the latter part of the nineteenth century and the earlier part of the twentieth mechanization, coupled with the agricultural depression, further weakened many villages, particularly those remote from urban centres. The process of rural depopulation has been as severe as that experienced during the later Middle Ages and resulted in the physical shrinkage and dereliction of many villages, particularly in the more isolated parts of the kingdom. On the other hand there were positive forces which often allowed villages to adapt to new opportunities or which led to the creation of new rural communities; most notably these were associated with industrialization and new modes of communication – the canal, the railway and, to a lesser extent, the turnpike road.

During this period villages changed radically, largely through their buildings; most of what we see today in our old villages dates from these comparatively recent centuries. It was not the great political events that directly influenced rural communities, although fortunes won from war or Empire were often expressed through a new house or park that would dramatically affect the fate of the village. Much more important were the underlying economic and technological changes that were eventually to lead to the virtual collapse of the village community in the twentieth century.

Nevertheless, between 1600 and 1900 many of the ancient villages were successfully adapted and rebuilt to meet changing conditions and even a few new villages were founded while others decayed or expired altogether. In the late sixteenth and early seventeenth centuries there was intense activity in many villages throughout the country and this period has been appropriately labelled 'the great rebuilding'. It saw the percolation of wealth through to the middle stratum of society and the expression of that prosperity in new buildings

129

both private and public. Many of the fine half-timbered houses of the West Midlands, misleadingly termed 'medieval', date from this period as do the limestone yeoman houses of the Cotswolds and the brick and flint mansions of eastern England. The great rebuilding also saw the construction of a range of public buildings – money which previously would have gone towards building or extending a church was used for constructing schools, markets and almshouses. Such altruism was not limited to towns and we find grammar schools such as Clipston built in 1667 and Guilsborough (1688) constructed in remote villages of Northamptonshire. In the north of England the rebuilding took place slightly later. In the Lake District, for instance, much new construction dates from after 1690. We should not underestimate the effect of this activity on both the visible features of villages and their topography. Rebuilding and construction are almost always associated with a redesign of the layout not only of individual dwellings but also of groups of houses and even whole communities. Much unrecorded alteration of village topography dates from this time.

This process continued intermittently throughout the eighteenth century – it is difficult to underestimate the scale of village replanning and rebuilding that went on during these two centuries. Not a single settlement in the country remained untouched and many, perhaps the majority, were substantially altered. Most of the planned villages were not new in that they were replacing already existing communities, but there were a number of completely fresh deliberate creations, for industrial, religious or political reasons, quite apart from a mass of new unplanned rural settlements of all shapes and sizes.

One difference between the medieval lord and his later counterpart was that the latter was often keen to set a distance between himself and his tenants, either by rebuilding his own dwelling on a new site, or more frequently by moving all or part of the village. The process of village movement in the post medieval period is most commonly associated with emparkment. In the late Middle Ages and even the sixteenth century the building of a great house and the making of an associated park often saw the total obliteration of the village without any attempt to recreate the community. Fawsley (Northants) is a good example of this, where the Knightly family, who acquired the estate at the beginning of the fifteenth century, evicted their tenants at the end of the century in order to build a fine Tudor mansion and create a new pastoral landscape out of their profits from the wool trade. Today there is no road to the church which sits amidst the earthworks of the village a few hundred metres from the ruined hall, overlooking a chain of landscaped lakes, the decaying remnants of the once fine park (see Fig. 21).

At Great Sandon in Staffordshire the Erdeswicke family owned a moated manor site at one end of the village, and in about 1600 they destroyed the village and emparked the village site. The present church of Sandon represents the former Little Sandon to which some of the dispossessed tenants migrated. The site of Great Sandon is still marked by the parish church, isolated in the park and by the deserted site of the old moated manor house below. During the seventeenth and eighteenth centuries more effort was made to rehouse at least some of the tenants, although if the emparkment involved the enclosure of arable, the removal of their livelihood must have meant that many were forced to leave whatever the squire's intentions. And in some cases emparkment was still carried out without making any alternative provision for the tenants. As late as the early nineteenth century the small township of Acton Reynold (Salop) was obliterated as part of a landscaping scheme without any attempt at resettling the community.

There are only a few well-documented examples of new villages in the seventeenth century, such as Sudbury (Derby) and the first stage of Great Tew (Oxon); the great age of village replacement was the eighteenth century. There are numerous examples of eighteenth- and nineteenth-century estate villages or settlements containing an estate element throughout the country. They are characterized by straight roads and uniform garden plots, often lying both in front and behind the houses. The houses of similar dimensions are normally semi-detached. The detailed architectural design of the houses rarely varies except in a systematic way – the

131

window and door mouldings are identical, except where there have been subsequent changes. In many respects such housing resembles pre- and immediately post-war local authority estate development, although the choice of building material and the passage of time means that such communities have tended to blend more naturally into the countryside. The nineteenth-century school will often occupy a separate unit at the end of the village and in later examples there may be a shop and post office incorporated in the scheme.

Initially many of these settlements were regular uniform rows on the edge of parkland, replacing old villages which had been obliterated in order to make way for an emparking scheme. Examples of this transference of population are to be seen everywhere in England in the form of uniform rows of cottages close to the entrance of a park. Nuneham Courtenay in Oxfordshire is perhaps the most celebrated example of this process, but numerous other cases could be cited. Another common feature is the retention of an ancient church within the park, either as a private chapel or as a landscape feature. At Nuneham Courtenay, commonly believed to be the 'Deserted Village' of Goldsmith's poem written in 1770, the village was removed from a bluff overlooking the River Thames to a new site on the Oxford-Henley turnpike road in the 1750s. In the early 1760s Goldsmith had actually witnessed the removal of an ancient village and the destruction of its farms in the making of a wealthy man's garden, some seventy-five kilometres from London. Nuneham Courtenay fits the description well and bears a striking resemblance to the poet's village of 'Sweet Auburn'. In the 'Deserted Village' Goldsmith expressed his fears that the destruction of villages and the use of productive land in the making of landscape gardens would bring ruin to the peasantry. Nuneham Courtenay was the work of the first Lord Harcourt who had a Palladian villa built over the old settlement, set in a park and designed on classical lines. To add insult to injury the lord, an atheist, had the medieval church pulled down and rebuilt as a classical temple to dovetail into his landscape design. For a century the parishioners of Nuneham had to walk the three kilometres through the park to attend services. A gloomy neo-Gothic church was eventually built close to the new village in 1880. Today the traffic thunders through on its way to and from Oxford, largely oblivious of this extraordinary demonstration of eighteenth-century baronial power.

During the seventeenth and early eighteenth centuries little imagination was used in the design of these settlements, but after about 1750 there were greater attempts to landscape the new villages and to plan them in a more sympathetic manner. From the 1770s there were pattern books available to land owners and surveyors creating new communities. Several early examples come from East Anglia. At Chippenham (Cambs), for instance, Edward Russell who had bought up two hundred hectares from five land holders, began work in 1696 and by 1712 half of the high street had disappeared inside the park and artificial lake. The new village consisted of fifty houses. The church and charity school were built of brick, while the single storey cottages were in pairs, in colour washed plaster and with tiled roofs, linked by outbuildings and with generous garden areas (Fig. 23).

The extent of new village building is difficult to estimate, ranging in scale from refacing or reconstruction of a small group of farm cottages through to the total rebuilding of a community. At Milton Abbas (Dorset), for example, Viscount Milton destroyed a sizeable market town, which included a market, grammar school, almshouses, shops, four inns and a brewery in order to make way for a new park around his house. This lay next to the splendid church of the Benedictine abbey which had been responsible for the foundation of the settlement in the first place. Between 1771 and 1790 Capability Brown and William Chambers were responsible for the total reconstruction of the settlement in the form of a sizeable model village some distance from the original town. In the park, which is a massive nine kilometres in circumference, the earthworks of the old town can be traced to the south of the abbey church. All the main streets are visible as well as most of the house sites. On the hillside the layout of the individual garden plots can also be identified. The new village included many of the features of the former town, but it was much smaller, and whereas the former community had been a

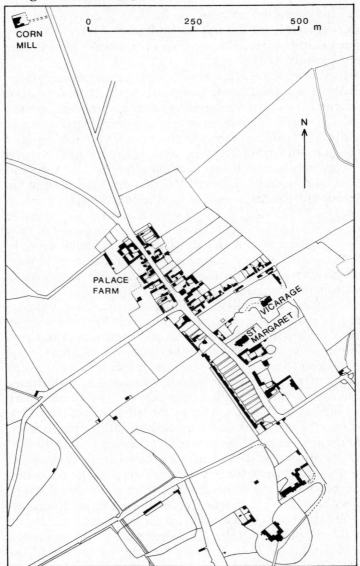

23. Chippenham, Cambridgeshire. An early example of a simple estate village, built about 1700 at the gates of Lord Orford's mansion.

prosperous one, the new downgraded settlement was over-crowded and relatively poor through the eventual loss of many of its market functions at Blandford Forum (Dorset). In recent years it has become a fashionable commuter and retirement village and the houses have been renovated – it is slightly ironic that a small block of council houses, where presumably most of the local workpeople live, has been tucked away well out of sight on a hillside to the north of the picturesque settlement (Fig. 24).

The style of reconstruction also varied immensely. At New Houghton (Norfolk), for example, Sir Robert Walpole constructed a new village consisting of ten sturdy two-storey cottages and almshouses in a simple brick style. Yet at Marford (Clwyd) a village was rebuilt in an eccentric Gothic style with ornamental window casements, curving roofs and walls; this was the work of an ambitious amateur, George Boskawen. Sometimes there was an attempt at conscious antiquarianism with inbuilt picturesqueness, use of thatch, bargeboards, latticed windows and chimneys. At Harlaxton (Lincs) the village was partially rebuilt and heavily restored in a picturesque style for De Ligney Gregory. One of the most eccentric villages was Edensor (Derby); here Capability Brown rebuilt the first village in about 1761, but in 1835 Joseph Paxton built a new village for the 6th Duke of Devonshire. The estate village was constructed in a wide selection of styles ranging from Swiss to castellated, out of sight of Chatsworth House.

The process of village creation continued well into the nineteenth century. In some instances Parliamentary enclosure appears to have acted as a stimulus. At Settrington (N. Yorks) the process of enclosure infringed on part of the old village, as the broad outgang was reduced to a roadway of normal width and most of the houses standing on the southern side were removed. While enclosure was in progress the lord, Sir Mark Sykes, was rebuilding both manor house and the village. Although a few of the old houses survive most of the remainder were rebuilt giving Settrington the spacious air of a planned estate village.

At Middleton Stoney (Oxon) the story was even more

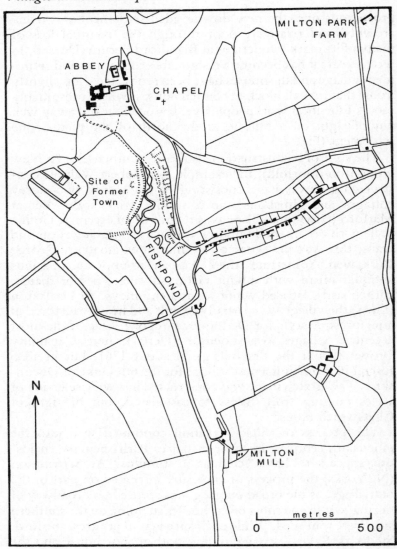

24. Milton Abbas, Dorset. One of the most celebrated examples of a transplanted settlement (1773–86). The extant model village was built by Lord Milton to replace the market town which originally stood in his park.

complicated and is a good illustration of the complexities of the mechanics of village morphology. The open fields were enclosed at the end of the seventeenth century and traces of the field boundaries shown on eighteenth-century estate maps can be seen as 'parchmarks' during dry weather within the park. In the early nineteenth century the 5th Earl of Jersey set about the expansion of the park and the extinction of the old village. The eastward extension of the park was completed in 1824–5, when the old manor house and adjoining cottages were demolished, leaving the church and castle mound isolated as a landscape spectacle, between the mansion and the park gates. New cottages were built on the edge of the park (now forming the nucleus of the present village) under the direction of Lady Jersey, the Countess Sophia. Each cottage had a rustic porch and a flower garden, conveying to one contemporary observer 'an idea of comfort and respectability seldom enjoyed by the working classes'. At East Stratton (Hants) there was a rather similar sequence of events. Stratton Park was enclosed by 1730 with the village lying outside the park. In 1801 Sir Francis Baring bought the estate and gradually extended the park; later in the nineteenth century the park was expanded to its present size and the village was rebuilt in conventional paired estate cottages just to the south-east of its former site. The church was also rebuilt.

There are numerous other examples dating to the first half of the nineteenth century, mainly to be found within a ninety-kilometre radius (or a day's coach ride) of London. In Oxfordshire, Heythrop Park was a late creation, with the model village and new church dating from the 1870s and 1880s. At Waddesdon (Bucks) an ambitious estate village, contemporary with Waddesdon Manor, was created by Baron Ferdinand de Rothschild. The new building included a hotel, institute, library and almshouses all in dark red brick. All the buildings carry the Rothschild emblem of five arrows, representing the baron's sons bound together in strength.

At Ripley (N. Yorks) the hall has dominated development; there is a triangular shaped cobbled 'square' in front of All Saint's, which is a large ornate church with chapel attached. The buildings are regulated, apparently all of similar construction in local stone with similar facings, window and door mouldings. The town was rebuilt in 1827–8 in Tudor style by Sir William Amcotts Ingleby, who replaced the old thatched houses with stone ones. There is an extraordinary Gothic Hotel de Ville, of 1854, towards the end of the village, which is now used as the post office. There is also a school of 1831 built in the form of a chapel.

Naturally enough it is in the countryside of large estates and country parks that such settlements are most commonly found. On the borders of Northamptonshire, Buckinghamshire and Oxfordshire, for instance, almost every village and hamlet is a planned one or contains an element of regulation. Here we can see the physical reality of the 'closed villages'. Cottisford, the 'Fordlow' of Flora Thompson's *Lark Rise to Candleford* (1939), contains many elements of estate planning. A mile or two to the north lies Mixbury (Oxon), a highly regulated village which lies along the road leading southwards from the church and the earthworks of a substantial medieval castle. This model village was created by order of the Court of Chancery as late as 1874 (Fig. 25) when the original stone and thatch cottages which were irregularly sited between the church and stream were replaced by semi-detached brick faced residences arranged in classic estate village formation. Just over the Northamptonshire border there is the village of Shalstone; here the church, manor house, rectory and manor farm lie within a parkland setting, quite apart from the rest of the community. The village has been cut off by emparking, and has a uniformity of design in many dwellings indicating strong development control – nineteenth-century replacement houses are particularly striking as being built to a pattern. The adjoining settlement at Biddlesden is a classic estate hamlet; the manor lies next to a landscaped fishpond and the small park is enclosed by a high wall, while outside lies a long terrace of brick cottages making up the present community. The chapel of St Margaret occupies one end of the stable block and is heavily disguised as a classical summer house. The list is far from complete as almost every settlement in the vicinity has been refashioned or completely rebuilt during the past two centuries. The sites of some of the earlier nucleated villages can

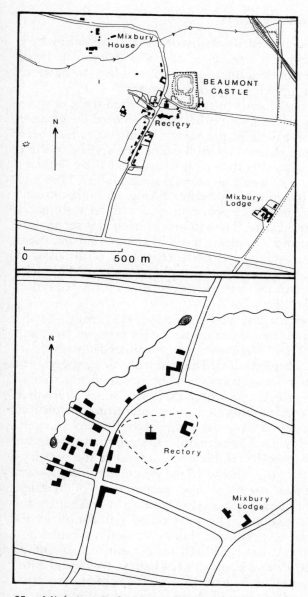

25. Mixbury, Oxfordshire. The bottom plan shows the settlement in 1823, it was destroyed and largely rebuilt by order of the Court of Chancery in the late nineteenth century.

sometimes be identified in earthwork form, but elsewhere elaborate emparking has removed all traces. However, ridge and furrow of sizeable dimensions is everywhere to be seen, both inside and outside the park enclosures.

Not all new settlements of this date resulted from emparking – the commercial incentive that had promoted the creation of so many new towns in the early Middle Ages had been rekindled in some places. One of the most interesting of these was Tremadoc (Gwynedd) which was founded by William Maddocks who purchased an area of poor land in 1798 and began a great reclamation scheme, taking an embankment across marshland to form a port principally aimed at shipping out locally quarried slate. The settlement itself was set against a sheer rock face and was planned round an open square; there was a town hall and a school complete with arcaded auditorium. The site was never completed because Maddocks went bankrupt, but the settlement remains a modest market centre to this day (Fig. 26).

Not all new settlements were planned so consciously – on the edge of woodland, fen and moor new communities were still being created. There were often uncoordinated squatter cottages and encroachments dotted haphazardly along the edge of wasteland, but in some instances they grouped together in small hamlets, particularly where there was some alternative form of industrial employment. An interesting pattern of settlements developed around the edge of the Somerset Levels; for instance, a dispersed linear hamlet has grown up along the back of the canalized River Tone at Curload in the parish of Stoke St Gregory. It is characterized by smallholdings, each with outbuildings used for the preparation of withies. Another new Somerset village was developed at Chantry for rather different reasons. The growth of population at six production centres persuaded James Fussell to build and endow a church at Chantry in 1846 'for the spiritual advantage of certain of the several parishes of Whatley, Mells and Elm, who reside at an inconvenient distance from their respective parish church and for whom there is no accommodation to attend divine service thereat' and it thereafter attracted a small permanent population. Mells incidentally had its own interest-

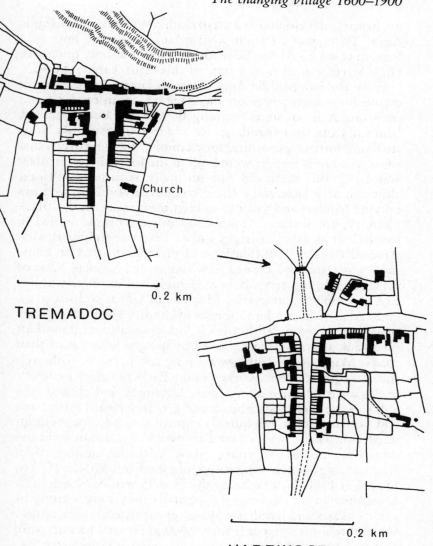

Church

0.2 km

TREMADOC

0.2 km

HAREWOOD

26. *Top*. Tremadoc, Gwynedd, founded by William Maddocks in 1798–1805 as a new commercial port. It failed because of a number of disasters. *Bottom*. Harewood, West Yorkshire, a formal estate and industrial village built at the gates of Harewood House for Edwin Lascelles.

141

ing history, developing as a small cloth town in the late Middle Ages. There was an attempt to rebuild it on the lines of a Roman town by Abbot Selwood, *c.* 1480, but only one road, High Street, survives as a relic of this remarkable scheme.

From the late Middle Ages onwards landless settlers were establishing themselves on the edge of common land and enclosing it as squatters, earning their living both from the land and from the expanding coal and iron industry. At Brigstock in Northamptonshire, for example, it was recorded that some forty new houses were built in the forest between 1600 and 1637. But these did not normally constitute villages, although at a later stage these conglomerations sometimes became hamlets and villages in their own right. In the Black Country, for instance, nailers and other workers settled in hamlets or isolated cottages rather than expanding towns. Around Brierley Hill (Staffs) coal miners squatted on common wasteland and created new unplanned hamlets. One of these, Delph, has recently been demolished to make way for fireclay mining, but nearby Mushroom Green still survives, embedded in the modern suburbs of Cradley Heath. It consists of early nineteenth-century brick cottages scattered at random on a bank above a stream, linked by hedged lanes rather than roads. Many of the cottages are long and narrow. Although the first squatters here worked in the Earl of Dudley's colliery at Saltwells, chain making soon developed and chainworks still survive there. Blackheath and Cradley Heath must have had similar origins, but quickly expanded to become medium sized industrial towns. West Bromwich, for instance, in the words of one contemporary, grew 'with the rapidity of an Illinois village', increasing its population from 5700 in 1801 to 65,000 in 1901. Not far away the Five Towns of North Staffordshire had similar origins; originally they were a group of poor villages and hamlets relying on subsistence agriculture, which began to prosper from *c.* 1600 as pottery manufacture and coal mining flourished. Burslem, the first to industrialize, developed out of a village grouped irregularly around a green.

In south Shropshire a group of squatter industrial villages grew around the Clee Hills. Bleak settlements such as Cleehill lie at over 350 metres above sea level on the open hillside as a tribute to man's tenacity. These communities were based on grazing and quarrying and never developed beyond small hamlets. Some ancient settlements were adapted to new industrial needs – villages such as Newbottle (Durham) have the appearance of mining communities with terraces of industrial houses. These, however, have been grafted on to a much older core, where even some of the earlier houses have been refaced to look like industrial dwellings. Similarly Nottinghamshire villages like Eastwood, D. H. Lawrence's childhood home, have been changed out of recognition by the development of coal mining. Some of the new rural mining communities were well designed, such as those on Earl Fitzwilliam's land in South Yorkshire. A report of 1842 of the Earl's mine at Elsecar describes the colliers' cottages in highly favourable terms and provides us with some insight into the mid nineteenth-century industrial village life.

> Those at Elsecar consist of four rooms and a pantry, a small back court, ash-pit, a pigsty, and a garden; the small space before the front door is walled round, and kept neat with flowers or paving stones; a low gate preventing the children from straying into the road. Proper conveniences are attached to every six or seven houses and kept perfectly clean. The gardens of 500 yards of ground each, are cultivated with much care. The rent for cottage and garden is two shillings a week. Each man can also hire an additional 300 yards for potato ground . . .

The village also contained a mechanics institute, library and school.

Throughout the kingdom small industrial communities were born or developed from the middle of the eighteenth century, from the china clay villages around Redruth in Cornwall to villages manufacturing paper, bricks and cement along the Thames estuary in North Kent. In many villages industry left hardly any trace. Examples are straw plaiting in eastern England, lace making in the south Midlands and framework knitting in Nottinghamshire. Often these activities were the relics of once-great industries, but they were still important for the survival of the village fabric. Much

143

industrial settlement was completely unplanned, or at least planned on a piecemeal basis, taking advantage of a mineral outcrop, a road junction or a canal terminal. Different industries gave rise to different patterns of housing. In Derbyshire, for instance, mining has been carried out by stake claims which meant that temporary ramshackle dwellings would be erected, or sheds converted into living quarters. Around mills tidier communities grew up, sometimes in the form of new settlements and sometimes on the basis of an old village.

The eighteenth century saw increasingly sophisticated attempts at creating model villages, both for agrarian and industrial purposes. Sometimes, the settlements were intended to incorporate both functions. At Harewood (W. Yorks) which lies on the main route down Wharfedale, a new community was grafted onto a much older one in the middle of the eighteenth century. The 1st Earl of Harewood had a house and new village built, the latter initially based on a ribbon factory that was designed to blend with the associated cottages. A nineteenth-century observer described the settlement thus: 'The whole of the town is built with fine stone procured from the neighbouring quarries and even the cottages possess a look of neatness bordering upon elegance, while the principal houses assume an air of superiority' (see Fig. 26). It should perhaps be added that the ribbon mill enjoyed only a short life and the nineteenth-century villagers found their principal employment in the house and estate. At Blanchland (Durham), the earls of Crewe created a new village for lead miners on the site of a Premonstratensian abbey and from its ruins constructed cottages of mellow sandstone (Plate VI).

The fashion for new industrial villages spread rapidly. At Cromford (Derby) Richard Arkwright designed a new settlement based upon his mill on the River Derwent in the late eighteenth century. The village was carefully planned with three-storey cottages and based on a central market place. The workers to house the village were moved out of Nottingham. Not far away at Rocester (Staffs), Arkwright established a cotton factory in 1781–2 called Tutbury Mill which still dominates east of the settlement, together with the workers' cottages, making the community an outstanding mill settlement of the Industrial Revolution.

The planned industrial village reached its zenith in the second half of the nineteenth century. The most ambitious venture was Saltaire, which lies on the River Aire about five kilometres from Bradford on the edge of the Yorkshire Moors. The scheme was the idea of Sir Titus Salt, one of the great northern industrial entrepreneurs. Saltaire was laid out on a grid pattern ignoring all geographical features except the river. It was founded in 1850, when 560 houses were grouped around a massive mill – when completed there was a church, chapel, dining rooms, a school house, lecture hall, almshouses and a laundry. It was an experiment in industrial sociology that was to have far-reaching consequences (Fig. 27). Saltaire possessed neither public houses, pawnshops nor police and provided the model for the Cadbury's at Bourneville and the Lever Brothers at Port Sunlight.

The village was a fertile ground for experiment by the reformer and, as early as 1696, John Bellars presented plans for an ideal village community to Parliament and subsequently many efforts were made to create what were considered perfect villages by their designers or sponsors. In the second half of the eighteenth century Moravian missionaries came to Britain and established seven new settlements. The most successful and best example of these is at Fulneck (near Pudsey in Yorkshire) which still survives as a religious community today. The village, built on the side of a hill in an extremely awkward position, consists basically of chapel with flanking housing and school. The members of the village carried out several trades including textile work (Fig. 27). Later Moravian villages were based on a square plan and built in a traditional eighteenth-century urban style, each one with a chapel marked by classical architecture, schools, houses for single brothers and sisters as well as other housing, shops and workshops. The schools became noted for a high standard of education.

Others were visionary in a different sort of way. Robert Owen was a philanthropist whose New Lanark was a bizarre attempt at the ideal community. Another radical movement

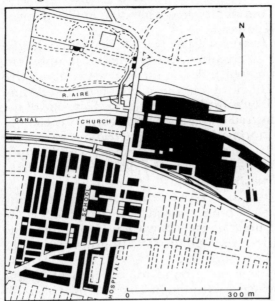

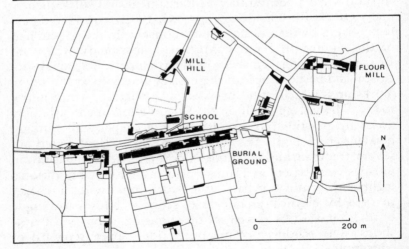

27. *Top*. Saltaire, West Yorkshire, near Bradford. One of the first and most ambitious industrial model villages, founded in 1850 by the Yorkshire philanthropist Sir Titus Salt. *Bottom*. Fulneck, West Yorkshire, was the first Moravian settlement, built on a difficult sloping site near Pudsey in 1748.

146

led to the development of the intermittently successful Chartist land colonies in 1846–50: Lowbands (Glos), Snigs End, Charterville, Minster Lovell, Gt Dodford (near Birmingham) (Fig. 28). This tradition continued at Whiteway (near Miserden, Glos) where a village colony was founded by a group of anarchists in 1898.

Another form of rural settlement that developed indirectly as a result of industrialization were the canal and railway settlements. During the eighteenth and nineteenth centuries thousands of miles of waterway and canal were constructed, often bypassing existing settlements and providing a new nucleus for building at a lock or halt. Often such hamlets became associated with nonconformity and had chapels of several denominations as well as small-scale industry. A good example of this is the growth of the hamlet of Newport (Humberside) along the Market Weighton Canal. At first, three adjoining groups of houses were separately known as New Gilberdyke (in Gilberdyke township), Newport (a township created at the enclosure of Wallingfen in 1781), and New Village (an extra-parochial district, also created in 1781); eventually the whole became known as Newport. By the 1850s there were several brickyards, a chicory kiln, a wind corn-mill, and a flax mill, while beside the turnpike road from Hull there were Wesleyan and Primitive Methodist chapels. More typical perhaps are very small communities such as Westport (Somerset) which sits at the end of the Westport canal, a canalized tributary of the River Isle. It consists of a large store warehouse, by the canal basin, and a large brick-built warehouse, as well as a number of new brick houses, an inn and a chapel. Similarly, Shardlow (Derby), another canal terminal village is characterized by warehouses, cottages and mills (Fig. 29).

One of the most famous canal settlements was Etruria (Staffs) which is now largely broken up by modern developments. The settlement lay on the Trent and Mersey Canal (1766–7) and Josiah Wedgwood bought an estate between Newcastle and Hanley through which the canal was being cut. In 1769 he proceeded to build a factory on its bank at the point where it was crossed by a turnpike road. This was followed by

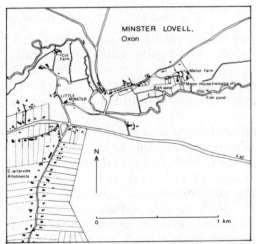

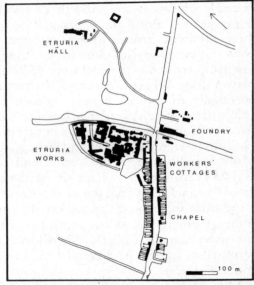

28. *Top*. Minster Lovell, Oxfordshire, has seen two phases of replanning, firstly in the late Middle Ages when a new regulated village was built to the west of the new manor house; and Charterville, a Chartist land colony, founded in 1847 to the south of the River Windrush. *Bottom*. Etruria, Staffordshire. In 1807 Josiah Wedgwood built a factory on the Trent and Mersey canal at the point where it was crossed by the Hanley-Newcastle turnpike. There followed a model village of workers' cottages along this road. The settlement is now much fragmented.

148

rows of model cottages for workers along the turnpike and a country house and park facing the factory across the canal (see Fig. 28).

The turnpike and enclosure roads, too, were responsible for refashioning some of the villages. For instance Benson (Oxon) lay on the Oxford–Henley–London turnpike and its broad open square surrounded by coaching inns is a direct result of it having been a stopping point during the eighteenth and nineteenth centuries. More normal was a subtle transference of a community from its ancient site to a position along a new road. At Luddington (Northants) there appears to have occurred complete village migration in the nineteenth century as a result of improved means of communication. The Parliamentary enclosure act of 1808 laid out a new road from Henington to Great Gidding, which replaced the old village high street. The village which had formerly lain on a damp site close to the Alconbury Brook, had a reputation for being 'low

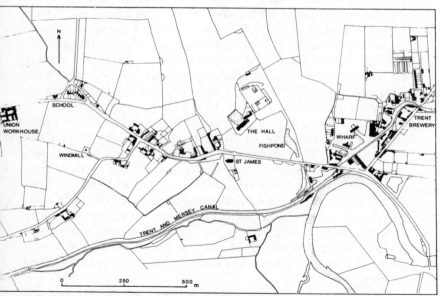

29. Shardlow, Derby. A settlement at the terminal of the Trent and Mersey canal, built between 1800 and 1815, it provided an alternative nucleus from the ancient village based on the parish church.

and dirty' and gradually took advantage of the new situation. In the middle years of the nineteenth century a number of buildings including the rectory, two farms and a number of cottages were demolished and new buildings constructed along the new road. Today Luddington in the Brook, as it was known, lies along the road and its old site is marked by an extensive spread of earthworks. Similar, if less dramatic examples could be cited from throughout the country, the creation of a new road in the nineteenth century almost always acted as a magnet to settlement, often resulting in the radical distortion of an ancient settlement plan.

Lord Palmerston shrewdly observed that 'the railways create station-houses and station-houses beget villages and little towns are springing up everywhere upon the lines of railways'. Between 1840 and 1850 the railway companies began constructing solid settlements – for instance New Wolverton and New Bradwell (Bucks) based upon a grid plan were sited on the road between Stony Stratford and Newport Pagnell at the point where the railway cut across the Grand Union Canal. The railway often influenced the settlement in quite surprising ways. On Dartmoor a small hamlet grew up at a halt at East Anstey, where there was an extensive market for sheep and ponies. The railway halt, the canal lock and the road junction all attracted a new type of settlement, often starting with an inn, followed by a chapel and cottages.

In the middle years of the nineteenth century villages probably had a greater diversity in form and economy than at any other time in their history. The new methods of transport were bringing cheaper building materials in the form of slate from north Wales and Cumberland and bricks from the eastern counties, and as a result many villages were given a facelift. Many villages were beginning to inherit some of the more attractive aspects of urbanization – reading rooms and halls of friendly and temperance societies, libraries, post offices, and shops without the attendant evils of poor housing and wicked working conditions.

Victorian piety ensured that the village church, which in the early years of the nineteenth century was often in a state of disrepair, was renovated and made sound for another century or so. New brick rectories and schools appeared and gave the outward appearance to the village of a firm stability.

We should not, however, fall into the trap of pastoral euphoria, as conditions in some unimproved settlements were still appalling. In 1850 Sir James Caird, *The Times* special agricultural commissioner, reported on Wark Castle in Northumberland. It was, he wrote:

> the very picture of slovenliness and neglect. Wretched houses piled here and there without order – filth of every kind scattered about or heaped up against the walls – horses, cows and pigs, lodged under the same roof with their owners, and entering by the same door – and many cases a pigsty beneath the only window of the dwelling – 300 people, 60 horses and 50 cows, besides hosts of pigs and poultry – such is the village of Wark.

Nevertheless if the future did not necessarily look bright everywhere, the village as an institution did at least appear to have a future. Country occupations were still thriving in 1851 when there were as many as 112,000 blacksmiths in Britain; most of them were employed in villages. Tuxford (Notts), for long a posting station on the Great North Road, in 1851 had saddlers, a tinker, an umbrella repairer, a ropemaker, coal merchants, a baker and home-made sweet shops – in addition to a chemist, vet and a lawyer. Even in the remote Lindwey Wolds, the village of Binbrooke (Lincs) could boast of 109 craftsmen, 31 tradesmen and 11 professional men out of a total population of just under 1300. If there were grounds for cautious optimism, they were soon to be sadly smashed. The apotheosis of the village during the period of Victorian confidence was to be short lived. Turnpike roads, canals and the railway conspired to break down country isolation and self sufficiency. From the middle of the nineteenth century the village community began to disintegrate. In Cerne Abbas, a large Dorset village not served by the railway, the fifty-seven tradesmen of 1851 had shrunk to a mere eleven by 1901. The decline of rural manufacturing both contributed to and resulted from the more general contraction of population in the countryside. As the number of agricultural workers decreased so the demand fell for the services of a wide range of craftsmen.

Added to this was the continued polarization of manufacturing industry in the towns. Industries which had once been widespread in the countryside occupied new locations at ports and major concentrations of urban population. Corn grinding, for example, one of the oldest forms of rural industry, ceased to be a truly rural activity during the last quarter of the nineteenth century as large mechanized mills were opened in towns to deal with home grown supplies, and in the ports to handle grain imported from overseas. In the 1880s some 160,000 chair-makers had been scattered throughout the Chiltern villages; within two decades the industry had become concentrated in the new factories in High Wycombe. Everywhere village industry and crafts were on the wane – the final phase in the life of the village as a coherent community had begun.

SELECT BIBLIOGRAPHY

Allison, K. J., *The East Riding of Yorkshire* (1976).
Darby, H. C. (ed.), *A New Historical Geography of England* (1973).
Darley, G., *Villages of Vision* (1975).
Hoskins, W. G., *The Making of the English Landscape* (1955).
Mingay, G. E., *Rural Life in Victorian England* (1977).
Palliser, D., *The Making of the English Landscape – Staffordshire* (1976).

7 Villages in decline – the Twentieth Century

The English village possesses great tenacity. Over the centuries it has proved to be an extremely flexible unit of settlement and its ability to survive into the late twentieth century is a mark of that tenacity. The 1894 Local Government Act preserved the village and parish as an element of local government with the establishment of civil parishes, which very closely followed the boundaries of the ancient ecclesiastical parishes. The 1974 Local Government Act recognized the parish as the bottom rung of democratic decision making in Britain. Despite this administrative recognition of the village as a place where people still dwell, the village as a recognizably independent form of settlement is all but dead – the village is now essentially an adjunct to the city.

The past century has seen dramatic developments in all aspects of life, and this has been reflected more slowly but perhaps more profoundly in the village scene than elsewhere. The modern village reflects the society in which we live, and as such is a cog within an extremely complicated interrelated administrative social and economic system. The village, as it has always been, is simply part of a much larger matrix. There are, of course, marked regional variations. The further one moves northwards or westwards, in pockets of East Anglia and Kent, one can still obtain a feeling of village life as it was a generation ago, or in some remote places even a century ago, but generally there has been an inexorable process of decay in the social and physical fabric of the village. The very basis on which the village flourished for thousands of years – agriculture and crafts – no longer play a serious part in the life of most rural communities. The basic stability that welded the village

153

population together through dramatic changes has now all but disappeared.

Throughout the twentieth century there have been two fundamental developments in British agriculture. Firstly a steady and relentless decline in the number of people involved in agricultural production since the late nineteenth century, to the point where today only 2.7 per cent of the population are employed in agriculture compared to 73 per cent of the land surface still in agricultural use. The second process which has accelerated since the last war is the application of technology to agriculture, resulting in the creation of an agricultural 'industry' which over much of the country is highly efficient.

The result of this has been that farm and village have become increasingly divorced from each other. It is true that this is a process which in some places started in the late Middle Ages, but it is now universal and has been heavily emphasized by the development of proficient mechanized farm complexes normally sited well away from the old rural communities. Thus the links between the farm and its land and the village community have been all but severed in many places. The farm now employs few if any local inhabitants and the farmer himself may be a professional manager with no links with the locality. The village and the locality have long since ceased to be the market for local farm produce, except perhaps for specialist products sold at the farm-gate to passing motorists; the farmer is part of a national, and since joining the Common Market, an international syndicate. There are still parts of the kingdom where villages and hamlets consist largely of working farms – though ironically this is more true now of pastoral areas in the north and west than the traditional arable lands of eastern and central Britain – but generally the number of farms operated from within the village framework has diminished, and is continuing to diminish. The rationalization of farming inevitably means that the industry will become progressively less labour intensive and therefore liable to be grouped in increasingly larger units.

The other principal form of village employment – craft-work – has now all but disappeared from the countryside. The process which had started in the late nineteenth century accelerated and by the last war there were very few village craftsmen still operating. Some people have looked to the village for a regeneration of local crafts, but although efforts have been worthy the scale of employment offered is minute. Employment opportunities in most villages are virtually nonexistent. In some areas there have been attempts to introduce light industry into the village, but generally speaking this has been on such a small scale that its impact has been minimal. More promising has been the development of villages for recreation and tourism; this does offer employment, albeit of a seasonal nature. The countryside is increasingly regarded by the town dweller more for its amenity value and less for its capacity to produce food. This latter development does underline the disquiet many people feel for the future of the village. Tourism is essentially transient and fluctuating and adds yet another impermanent ingredient to village life.

Up until the last war village England was in a state of physical deline. Agriculture was at a very low ebb and job opportunities within the community were strictly limited, so the process of migration from many rural areas which had started in the nineteenth century continued unchecked. Against this, however, should be set the fact that most of the village institutions were still functioning, and very many rural communities still included at least one flourishing religious building quite apart from their parish church. Many villages could boast of a school and often a Sunday School, shops, a post office, a baker and often carpenter, shoemaker, and tailor, quite apart from builders, saddlers, blacksmiths and so on. Nevertheless all these reflected a former stability and way of life that was declining quickly – a decline that was accelerated by the war.

Ironically, since the war many villages have experienced a new upsurge of vitality, while at the same time witnessing a dramatic fall in the number of available services. Increased mobility, through the motorcar and, to a lesser extent, public transport, has meant that many services that were previously provided in each village are now available only in the nearest town or in a key village chosen because of its central position. The local store and post office have followed the school to the

155

market town, and parish churches are being made redundant at the rate of about one hundred a year.

The village has thus both suffered and benefited as a result of this increased personal mobility; there has been a profound change in work patterns – many people are now prepared, and able, to travel considerable distances to their places of work. This started with the development of the railway network at the end of the last century around London, but has since spread to cities and towns throughout the land (Fig. 30).

Between 1951 and 1971 there has been an increase of about 25 per cent in the rural population, and today almost one-fifth of the population lives in rural settlements. Against this, however, should be noted that although the national trend is one of growth in rural areas, almost a third of all rural districts are continuing to lose population, these of course tending to be in the western, less accessible parts of the country. The reason for the overall increase in population is of course increased mobility through the motorcar. Villages which lie within thirty kilometres of a town or an employment centre have been taken up as pleasant places to live in and this is reflected everywhere in the rebuilding and renovation of houses, house-extensions, single and double garages, infilling and village expansion.

We have only to look at those villages which lie close to large urban centres in southern England to see this process of change in our own lifetimes. Since the second world war many of these settlements have been chosen, or more often because of close proximity to a town, have evolved, as nuclei for commuter development. Private and council estates have been grafted onto ancient centres, in many cases changing the character of the original village out of all recognition. In some cases a new road has bypassed the old village centre and acted as a focus for development, while in others the development has joined old villages to an outward spreading conurbation – a process that occurred in the eighteenth and nineteenth centuries in places like London and Birmingham but has continued at an accelerated rate around many towns and cities in the twentieth century. If we look at Nottingham, for instance, we see that the former separate villages of Burton Joyce,

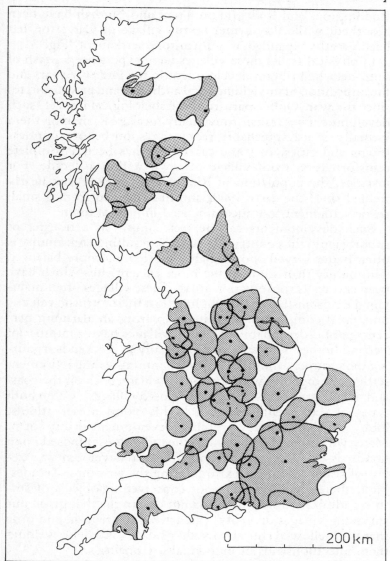

0   200 km

30.   Plan showing the areas from which commuters were drawn in 1961. Since the expansion of the motorway and trunk road network there are few parts of the country which lie outside the commuter zone.

157

Ruddington, and Radcliffe on Trent and Nuthall have been absorbed, while the former textile village of Calverton has been greatly expanded as a dormitory settlement (Fig. 31).

In physical terms these villages have experienced a rash of semi-detached ribbon development in the interwar years and the imposition of unyielding local authority and private estates since the war. Quite apart from the sociological impact, such development has transformed many rural areas, making them virtually indistinguishable from the suburbs of countless towns and cities. In some cases there has been a complete transformation from village to town within a decade. For instance, the population of Ringmer (E. Sussex) has nearly trebled since the early 1960s and has changed from a small rustic settlement to a medium sized industrial town.

Such developments can be seen simply as a transfer of suburbia into the countryside, and the resulting community is often better served and probably therefore a more balanced community than some of the more ancient sites which have been chosen as conservation areas. These villages often maintain their ostensible charm but have lost their intrinsic value as integrated communities. Quite apart from an alarming percentage of older inhabitants many villages have a number of 'second homes' normally occupied only at weekends or during the summer months. The pretty commuter and retirement settlement together with the tourist village both on the coast and inland have become the new 'closed villages'. Often both types of settlement contain a highly vocal preservationist lobby which effectively prohibits development in any form. Many will applaud and point to the indignities imposed upon hundreds of villages by unsympathetic redevelopment careless of scale, colour or texture during the past three decades. Nevertheless villages were not conceived as objects of aesthetic admiration; it is time and not design that has given our surviving villages diversity, character and strength, and time that has mellowed church, dwellings, lanes and field, welding them into thousands of individual personalities.

Our problem is not change, for we have seen that in the end change is essential for the survival of the village, rather it is the scale and nature of change that needs to be monitored in order

to conserve our villages. The village cannot survive as a fossilized museum piece, it must have a functional role otherwise
eventually it will die away. As one pessimistic observer has
recently written, 'Villages are rapidly becoming ghettos of the
elderly, housebound and the wealthy.' Yet another category
of village consists of those that have outlived their usefulness
and cannot find alternative functions. Predominantly these are
situated in areas of continued rural depopulation and the unat-
tractive rural settlements of the industrial revolution. It has
been the policy of at least one local authority – County
Durham – to encourage the disappearance of a sizeable percentage of these villages in the jargon terminology 'at the end of
the life of the building stock' (Plate XIX).

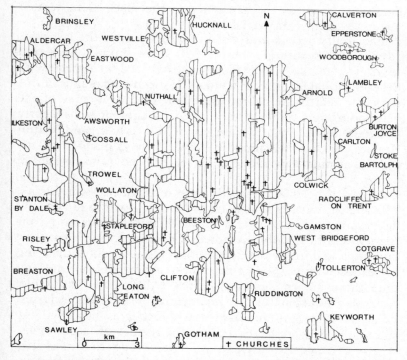

31.   Plan showing the incorporation of outlying villages in the framework
of suburban Nottingham. Each church represents an ancient village nucleus.

159

Yet the imagery of the village is still potent, perhaps never more so than today. In the 1930s the term 'garden village' was widely applied to all housing schemes, wherever their location. After the war there was a spate of literature by planners and sociologists who saw the village as one of the solutions for a better life, and writers like Thomas Sharp who, in his *Anatomy of the Village* (1946), promoted the village as being highly relevant for the creation of new communities. There have been few new villages built since the war but Sharp was given the job of planning a number of villages for the Forestry Commision, on the remote borders of Scotland and England. These illustrate graphically the short fall between the ideals of the most enlightened planners and the numerous intervening factors which can so easily invalidate the best of schemes. The details to improve the aesthetics of the place seem wasted effort set against the social realities.

The Reilly plan published immediately after the last war, advocated a seemingly simple device for linking areas of a town, treating each as a village centre, based on a green with the communal facilities at hand. The social advantages of this were the real point behind the plan, the advantages of the neighbourhood unit, or the linked villages of the recently designed new towns, Washington (Co. Durham) and Milton Keynes (Bucks). Washington New Town is planned on the system of nineteen village units, each to be quite distinct in design.

Milton Keynes is presented with more difficult problems. The ancient villages which are to be consumed in the general development will inevitably lose their functions and continuity will be totally disrupted. Older and more attractive buildings will immediately take on a higher value, appearing as islands within a sea of new mass-produced housing, and thus these ancient village centres will become desirable, expensive housing for the managerial, professional classes. Precisely the same about-turn will occur as has been the case in countless villages around the fringes of larger cities, where a desperate attempt is being made to preserve a superficial resemblance to the country communities they were once.

Villages in decline – the Twentieth Century

Today we can identify three broad categories of village. The suburban commuter village, the conservation and tourist village, and the decaying village. As always, there will not be rigid boundaries between these categories and some settlements will contain characteristics of two or even all three forms. Although the village as a social and economic unit is all but dead over much of Britain, it does persist as a geographical entity. The physical village contains a wealth of archaeological, historical and architectural resources, and these should not be squandered. Nevertheless, villages cannot live solely on the basis of their past, but must have a function to play in the modern world if they are to survive in a recognizable form to the end of the twenty-first century.

SELECT BIBLIOGRAPHY

Clout, H. D., *Rural Geography an Introductory Survey* (1972).
Darley, G., *Villages of Vision* (1975).
Moss, G., 'The Village: a matter of life or death', *Architects' Journal*, 18 January (1978).
Sharp, T., *The Anatomy of the Village* (1966).
Woodruffe, B. J., *Rural Settlement Policies and Plans* (1976).

8 Fieldwork and the village

Archaeologists spend a great deal of time uncovering the surviving traces of early communities through the process of excavation, and historians using documentary evidence are able to reconstruct a wide variety of aspects of past village life. Yet until recently the village itself has been neglected as a source of historical information; however, largely as a result of work by pioneer landscape historians such as Professor W. G. Hoskins and Professor M. Beresford, there has been increasing interest in the fabric, layout and organization of surviving settlements. The analysis of villages for historical and planning purposes is still in its infancy, but the danger to surviving rural settlements is such that it is necessary to formulate some fieldwork approaches as a matter of urgency.

We have at our disposal a vast quantity of information on which to base our study of villages and village plans. Naturally the further one goes back in time the less settlements are related to the existing landscape framework and therefore they are more difficult to analyse. We have seen that settlements rarely remain completely static for very long and even a single century can witness significant changes. There are, however, advantages in this constant shift of village plan in that only the areas occupied by the most recent habitations are normally not available for study. By collecting surface artefacts, examining earthworks, excavating sites of different periods and using documents as evidence, a relatively clear picture of the evolution of individual villages and of rural settlement within an area can often be obtained as far back as the late Saxon period and in some cases earlier.

It is necessary to analyse the physical evidence in order to understand the development of the village. Just as archaeologists examine the vertical stratification of debris left by previous generations the fieldworker must survey the standing structures, try to analyse relationships and work out a chronology for the settlement. Recent developments need to be distinguished from the more ancient elements within the village, although sometimes modern houses are simply replacing older structures or are infilling gaps which have developed over the years, and brick or stone casings often encase older timber-framed buildings. Many villages, particularly in the north, have experienced a phase of industrialization and this may have completely masked the older settlement pattern; it may be reflected by a fragmented settlement pattern, with strings of terraced houses distributed irregularly over a mineral outcrop.

If the village has begun to decay what features are there to look for? One obvious indication is the presence of derelict buildings. In some conditions the evidence from decayed buildings will survive much longer; thus it is not uncommon to find surface traces of stone dwellings still standing in upland heath areas. For instance, a few years ago the stone base of a complete medieval village was found overgrown with heather at Hound Tor on Dartmoor. However, it is far more common to find evidence of decayed houses in the form of earthworks, where the buildings have been reduced to low platforms over which turf has formed. It is also possible to identify abandoned areas of occupation within surviving villages in the form of empty tenement plots. Sometimes these reflect a considerable reduction in the size of the community, while in others the settlement has simply shifted and houses have been rebuilt on a new site elsewhere.

The final stage in the process of decay is the abandonment of the complete settlement. Such sites can be identified in a number of ways – they may be in the form of earthworks describing the site of former occupation. Hundreds of medieval and prehistoric villages survive in earthwork form and a number of Romano-British and earlier sites have recently been identified. In areas where stone or brick were the principal construction materials, well-defined building platforms are often found. In areas when timber and clay were mainly employed, the sites of former dwellings will be less distinct, but in some cases earthworks will reflect the build up of soil and debris outside the walls of the building. Apart from the buildings themselves it is often possible to distinguish the lines of property boundaries in the form of linear banks, roads in the form of hollow ways and of the associated fields in the form of ridge and furrow or rectangular boundaries.

Empty tenement blocks should be examined for earthworks and the areas around the extant village should be carefully inspected to see if there is evidence of former occupation. The relationship between surviving buildings and earthworks can be a complicated one, ranging from very small-scale earthworks resulting from a minor shift of emphasis, through to almost complete desertion with only a very few houses sitting amidst a considerable area of irregular earthworks (Plate XX). Plate XXI, for instance, shows Ludborough (Lincs) with empty tenement blocks represented in earthwork form situated within the surviving village. It also shows an impressive fishpond complex just above the village, and how the modern road virtually bypasses the village, isolating the old main village street. In such cases it is important to identify those surviving buildings which could have been contemporary with the abandoned settlement sites. Are we looking at the final stages of village abandonment or are those buildings which survive, with the possible exception of the parish church, created after the abandonment of the village? Are we in fact looking at a resettlement?

Where part or whole of the former settlement will have been ploughed, levelled or built over, the fieldworker must rely upon the presence of surface artefacts or differences in soil colours indicating buried features. It is necessary to walk the fields when freshly ploughed to look for concentrations of pottery, bone and flints which may indicate former occupation sites. Conventional fieldwalking techniques are sufficient to identify such sites, however, except in cases where ploughing has only recently destroyed the surface earthworks, when it is rarely possible to understand the geography of the former settlement. Aerial photography may well help at this stage –

the whole layout of the village may be clearly demarcated in cropmarks or soilmarks intelligible only from the air.

Preparing for fieldwork

Before visiting the village the fieldworker should obtain a large-scale map of the inhabited area. The os six inch map (currently being replaced by the 1 : 10,000) will provide a general plan of the site together with information about extant buildings, property boundaries and roads. However, if a detailed examination is to be undertaken the os twenty-five inch map (1 : 2500) is essential. This is on a scale large enough to allow the annotation of features, and the comparative analysis of such elements as tenement frontages and building materials. If possible when visiting a site several copies of the plan should be available in order to record buildings of different periods, styles and fabrics, or features such as field- and road-names or areas of earthworks. Copies of earlier village maps should be obtained and reproduced at a common scale so that changes in village morphology can be easily identified. In addition there will often be etchings, watercolours and early photographs, all of which can contain valuable topographical information.

Before visiting the village the fieldworker should also acquaint himself with some knowledge of the village history from documentary sources. In many cases there will be some form of printed history, for some areas there will be a parish and manorial history included in the relevant volume of the *Victoria County History*. The more recent volumes of the *V.C.H.* are particularly valuable as they normally contain details of local economic history in addition to a wide range of information about the administration, social life and topography of the village. In other areas there will be the writings of local antiquaries, although accuracy, relevance and detail will inevitably vary greatly. It is particularly important to obtain some ideas about the history of land ownership in the parish; for instance if there was a large estate operating in or near the settlement, it will almost certainly have influenced the topography of that settlement.

165

Although individual rural buildings have received considerable attention in the past, there have been few systematic attempts at village analysis by archaeologists or historians. However, the pressure for redevelopment has resulted in the need to assess the archaeological and historical value of villages in areas of population pressure, where infilling and expansion are most likely. Such historical assessments are essential if we are not to lose the vast majority of surviving villages without record in the next half century. One of the first attempts at village analysis has been in the area around Bristol where the Committee for Rescue Archaeology in Avon, Gloucestershire and Somerset have produced a format for rapid village survey (Appendix 1). Although a technique of this type naturally has deficiencies its value lies in the speed with which it can be applied to a large number of comparable rural communities, in order that conservation priorities can be decided upon.

The village site and plan

The fieldworker should examine the site occupied by the village from the point of view of geology, soils, communications and the availability of water. In the case of an extant village, there may be documents, place- or field-names, earthworks or even folk memory which would suggest that the settlement has previously occupied a different or a larger area. If it can be demonstrated that the village has moved there may be obvious geographical or economic reasons which will account for the shift. One of the most common reasons for a shift of settlement is the creation of a new road bypassing the ancient core of the village. This often attracts new development leading to the abandonment of the more ancient area of occupation.

The careful analysis of village plans and field evidence often enables a well-defined layout of roads and houses to be identified. Such regular villages have been discussed above (see Chapter 2). Attention should be paid to existing or former village greens; the pattern of roadways, particularly the existence of back lanes and service roads; the relationship of the main habitation area to the church and to the manor house. If

166

Fieldwork and the village

these two major buildings are divorced from the main village then there has probably been movement or regulation. Most settlements of any size are composite structures where it is possible to distinguish more than one element in the village plan; there are often linear and green units within the same settlement (Plate XXII). Separate sections of villages frequently carry their own names, for instance, 'Town End', 'the Township', or 'Church End'. A particular characteristic of the Midlands is the name 'London End' or 'City End' in that part of the village lying on the road leading outwards towards London. Cold Higham (Northants) consists of three quite distinct and separate units, all of which are covered by the same village name – a preliminary examination will often provide a working hypothesis on which the village can then be examined. This is valuable even if the theory has to be discarded upon investigation of the ground evidence.

Is there an obvious water supply in the form of a spring, village pond, well or stream and how does the layout of the village relate to this supply? In areas of porous rock, settlements have tended to concentrate sources of water as a large number of remote villages have been served with mains water only in the post-war era. Thus in upland limestone areas villages have frequently been tightly nucleated, based on a spring or well.

Is there any trace of a village boundary where the gardens and closes give way to agriculture? These are often clearly seen in earthwork form on the sites of deserted villages, but they can also be traced in surviving settlements either as a bank and ditch or simply marked by a wall or fence. Outside the settlement the characteristic earthwork of ridge and furrow will mark the area of former arable cultivation.

Roads

The village roads are most likely to determine the 'grain' of the settlement and should therefore be carefully examined, particularly those which serve the village from outside. Where do they come from, are they linking the settlement with other villages, are they simply field lanes serving the local farms, and

167

where do they actually enter the built-up area? Are there any obvious diversions or bypasses? The road used by through traffic today may well be quite modern and miss the nucleus of the village. At Stoke Doyle (Northants) extensive earthworks indicate the gradual movement of the village from its original valley-bottom site to the present north-south through road from Oundle to Aldwincle. Alternatively it may have been moved deliberately when the former manor house was built. The aerial photograph of Monington (Hereford & Worcester) shows how the road has been diverted around a field to approach the church. The former road is identifiable as a soil mark (Plate XXIII).

The presence of an ancient cul de sac can be informative; is there an obvious reason why roads should have been blocked, is it an isolated example or part of a pattern which will show that a dominant authority has influenced the village plan? Are there any roads running at variance to the general trend, and if so are there any obvious explanations? Units of eighteenth- and nineteenth-century industrial housing, grafted onto a more ancient settlement, often portray this characteristic, occupying odd segments of land bought up by entrepreneurs to house as many people as possible. Large-scale maps will show the siting of old trackways as well as extant communications – it is important to locate route junctions outside the present village. This sometimes indicates the site of an earlier settlement centre which has subsequently been replaced. At Clun (Salop), for instance, the ancient roads converge on the church of St Michael to the south of the River Clun. Most of the settlement today, however, lies to the north of the river, laid out in the form of a small bastide town in the shadow of a massive earthwork castle. It is quite clear that the settlement was replanned in the early Middle Ages leaving the ancient village centre in isolation (Plate XXIV).

The church

Probably the best place to start the assessment of most villages is with the parish church or ancient chapel. The church will normally be the oldest standing structure in the village, and

168

will embody the whole development of the village, sometimes right through from the late Anglo-Saxon period. Is there any evidence that it was a pre-Norman minster church or was it founded after the Conquest? Such evidence may survive in architectural or documentary form. The omission of a reference to a church in Domesday Book does not necessarily mean that there was not a church there in the eleventh century. Is there any suggestion that the church started as a chapel dependant upon a mother church? If so, it may throw some broader light upon the origins of the settlement pattern in the area. In some instances it is possible to reconstruct large ancient parish estates by identifying chapelries belonging to an original church; the territories served by these chapels often formed a large multiple estate.

Attention should be paid to the church dedication – this may be linked with Saxon saints and thus suggest an early foundation. In the vicinity of the Roman town of Viriconium (Salop) there are a number of churches which were originally dedicated to early saints. The church at Atcham has a unique dedication to St Eata (died AD 685), a companion to St Aidan. Nearby at Cressage the ancient, now destroyed church, was dedicated to St Samson from Wales (died ?AD 565).

Some, such as those named after St Michael, St Catherine and St Edward often appear to have been associated with islands of higher ground and high places. During the Middle Ages it was quite common to change the dedication, but it may be possible to identify the original saint by identifying the parochial festival day when it does not coincide with that of the saint's day. The Roman calendar will help in limiting the number of possible saints to whom the church was originally dedicated, thus helping to find out when the church was first constructed on the site.

The site occupied by the church and its relationship to the surrounding area should be examined. For instance, does it occupy the highest point in the village? If so, then it is likely to be an early feature; but in some cases it can be demonstrated that the church was a late arrival and sited on the edge of an existing settlement. Examples where this can be convincingly demonstrated are rare, as in many cases the relationship between the church and the village cannot be determined by observation or even documentation. In the case of Long Stanton (Salop), however, the small parish church lies on a slope a little distance away from the now depleted linear settlement. We know that it was only a chapel in the early Middle Ages and therefore it is safe to assume that the church came after the establishment of a settlement here, and was forced to occupy a site outside the main village.

A church lying divorced from the modern village may, however, simply represent a shift in the settlement itself. In some cases the church will occupy a croft within a regular village plan, which will probably date from a period of reorganization or regulation. In such cases the churchyard will conform to the general pattern of property boundaries within the settlement (see Appendix 1). In such cases this may have been the first church here or it may have been moved in order to accommodate the new village plan. This emphasizes that the church site was not perhaps as sacrosanct as we have been. If the church is predominantly Romanesque, it is quite likely that the village has lacked the funds to rebuild and has remained relatively poor since the Middle Ages. In the Welsh borderland there are many small Norman churches, for instance Rock (Worcs) and Heath (Salop) which have been attached to poor scattered communities and have hardly been altered since they were originally constructed. Conversely, if there are major additions in the form of aisles or perhaps a tower, these may point to periods of prosperity which can be related to a former wealthy patron, trade or industry. Many churches were often extended or completely rebuilt by patrons who grew rich on some local source of wealth such as the wool trade. In such cases it is often possible to identify a dominant style attributable to a period of prosperity; sometimes interior brasses or monuments can help to elucidate this. If a parish church is more elaborate than its neighbours, if it has transepts or contains more ornamentation, the cause is normally to be found in a wealthy patron. Alternatively, is there any evidence for the church having contracted, perhaps in the form of blocked aisles or blocked doorways, which might illustrate a period of local economic decline.

170

The great Victorian era of church rebuilding and renovation removed much of this valuable information and effectively sterilized many church interiors. However, certain features such as ornamental brasses will have survived and sometimes medieval features will have been imitated by the nineteenth-century architects. For example, the Earl of Jersey completely dismantled the church tower at Middleton Stoney (Oxon) in 1855 but the new tower was rebuilt in precisely the same Norman transitional style as the original structure. The very failure of the Victorians to renovate a particular church can in itself be of interest, indicating perhaps a less successful parish. If the church is a post-medieval building, does it contain any older features such as a font or reused masonry from an earlier church which may have stood on the site?

Most medieval churches are entered by the south door, there may be a corresponding north door designed originally for processional use and perhaps also a grand west door at the base of the tower. But unless there is an obvious practical reason the normal entrance is from the south, so that if a church has an entrance in an alternative position, the reason for this location should be sought. In the case of Marston Magna (Somerset) the southern entrance has been blocked up and a modest doorway inserted in the north aisle. In the surrounding fields the earthworks of a large moated manor house together with house platforms of a former settlement can be seen. It is clear that the village now lies to the north-west of the church and the change in the siting of the door simply reflects easy access from the now shifted settlement.

In the Middle Ages much business was enacted outside the church doorway and church porches often contained an altar at which contracts could be signed. At South Poole (Devon) a stone bench which runs along the east wall of the church is raised in the centre to form an altar table. Even where the actual porch altar has vanished, proof of its former existence can be seen in the irregular placing of the doors of late Saxon porches at Bradford-upon-Avon (Wilts) and Bishops Stow (W. Sussex). From the late fourteenth century onwards porches with an upper storey became common and such business that had formerly been transacted in the porch was transferred to the chamber above. Such grand entrances, however, are not common in the English parish church and where they are found in a village they often reflect a former prosperity, and often indicate a degree of urbanization.

Some churchyards contain complete or fragments of medieval crosses, which may originally have been secular in function. The size of the cross, irrespective of its location, may well give some indication of the market pretensions of a settlement. In the case of Castle Rising (Norfolk) a monumental village cross indicates its former importance as a small trading town connected to the sea by long silted-up channels. Similarly at Hinton St George (Somerset) a large village cross is situated in what appears to be an eighteenth-century estate village, but analysis of the street plan shows that it originally stood at the head of a sizeable green.

The manor house

Next to the church the manor house or hall-garth is the most common large building in the community. Originally the lord's house may have been barely distinguishable from the other village dwellings, that is of course unless it was fortified or moated. From the fifteenth century onwards, however, the house in which the lord or squire resided was rebuilt and often resited, normally resulting in a reshaping of the village in the form we see today. There was a tendency to create, in the richer parts of the country at least, elaborate country houses to replace the older, more humble, manor houses. When this happened it was often associated with the creation or extension of a landscaped park. For instance, to the north of Woodstock (Oxon), a whole group of villages were dramatically changed by emparking during the seventeenth to nineteenth centuries, perhaps resulting from the example of the adjacent Blenheim great park. Villages such as Kirtlington, Wootton and Yarnton have virtually been displaced by extensive emparking and the incorporation of the parish church as within a new landscaped environment.

At Hinton St George (Somerset) the initial creation of a large landscaped park does not appear to have influenced the actual shape of the village. However, in the eighteenth and nineteenth centuries there seems to have been a deliberate attempt to give the settlement the appearance of a model village. This was done by refacing many of the houses in a similar style and by selective hedge and tree planting. The construction of an eighteenth-century rectory near the church seems to have been used as an excuse to landscape the core of the village, including the church itself.

In many cases, such developments lead to the partial or complete destruction of village life. There were numerous instances where the village in front of the house was levelled off either for landscape gardening or simply to create an open space; for instance at Morville (Salop), where the Norman church of St Gregory stands alone in the middle of a field, overlooked by Morville Hall, while the present hamlet lies along a diverted road to the south-east of the Hall. At Coughton Court (Warwicks) the impressive sixteenth-century manor house was inserted next to the church causing the village to be uprooted, so that the settlement now lies some 500 metres away along the line of a diverted road. At Minster Lovell (Oxon) the construction of an ambitious late medieval manor house appears to have led to the complete displacement of the village and its reconstruction in a model linear form some 500 metres to the west of the church and manor house. It is ironic that a much later attempt at village plantation – a mid nineteenth-century Chartist settlement – should also have been at Minster Lovell and should have met with such modest success (see Fig. 28). Such examples can be cited from throughout the country and emphasize the importance played by the power of the lord of the manor in fashioning the shapes of our villages. Frequently the creation of a large house and park will have obliterated all earlier traces of the village which they have replaced. Village earthworks or parchmarks of underlying buildings are frequently to be found in parklands, close to the great house.

One should also consider those features which were often associated with manor houses. Landscaped gardens originated in the late Middle Ages and sometimes survive in earthwork form as terraces, depressions and ditches. Stone dovecotes,

173

normally circular in shape, are another commonly found surviving feature of the manor. Traces of fishponds are also to be found in the form of strings of rectangular ponds still holding water or the earthwork dams which have normally been breached leaving behind a series of marshy hollows. Sometimes the manor house itself will have disappeared, and in many cases it will have left earthwork traces behind, often in the form of a sizeable platform or a moated site. Sometimes such remains can be detected amongst ordinary house earthworks or fishponds.

Other buildings

Relatively few lesser medieval buildings survive today. In the sixteenth and early seventeenth centuries the 'great rebuilding' saw the removal or remodelling of most medieval houses and associated structures, since then there have been repeated alterations and rebuildings throughout the country. Buildings which have been legally protected or 'listed' should be identified, but it ought to be remembered that such lists are often meaningless as a reflection of the wealth of historic architecture in a settlement.

To understand the often complicated history of ordinary dwelling houses is difficult without experience, often involving the production of detailed drawings. Village buildings, especially those over a century old, have been subject to constant change in the form of addition, subtraction, refacing, reroofing or amalgamation. Often the true story of the history of a building can only be traced through the interpretation of subtle changes which are reflected in the roof timbers. Nevertheless the fieldworker can make some initial observations about several features, including the position of the dwelling within the village layout, the main building styles found within the settlement and the range of building functions. There are a number of fieldwork guides which can help with this survey (see Select Bibliography.)

Firstly, the house site should be examined. How do the buildings stand, in relation to their own enclosures, and to central or subsidiary roads on which they sit? Which way are the houses facing – away from the main street or in a variety of different directions? Is there an obvious reason for this, perhaps in the form of a blocked-in lane which used to serve them? Is there any inter-communication between the various houses – are they detached, semi-detached or terraced? All of these points should be taken into account when trying to understand the development of the village. In some cases the original dwelling will have been destroyed leaving only secondary buildings such as barns or stables.

What of the building styles in the village? Normally speaking these will not vary greatly from contemporary town buildings. Often, however, there will be nothing particularly elaborate, and as rural styles are often slower to change than those in towns it is not uncommon to find building styles being employed in villages that have long since been superseded in urban centres. Attention should again be paid to the unusual and the ambiguous and to whether all the buildings appear to be of the same date, as for instance in an estate village (see Plate VI). Is this because they were all built at the same time or because there has been an attempt to make them look similar? For instance, the small village of Acton Burnell (Salop) appears to consist of a whole series of similarly rendered houses. This was, however, an attempt at regulation in the nineteenth century; the cores of many of the buildings are in fact far older.

What are the building materials used in the construction of the houses? Is it local stone, brick or is it mainly timber in the older houses? It is particularly valuable to locate the source of building stone in areas where it does not occur naturally. Occasionally stone for domestic buildings will have been taken from a nearby monastic ruin, castle or decayed manor house. In such cases, blocks of more elaborate superior stonework should be looked for. If brick has been used, was it produced locally and is it possible to date the period of manufacture? Has the building been refaced with stone or brick? (At certain periods brick has been more fashionable than stone or timber, therefore we sometimes find brick facades added to buildings of an otherwise different material.) It does not necessarily mean that a facade is later than the original buildings.

175

For instance, in the stone-hungry area of the Upper Thames Valley some of the finer buildings are constructed of imported limestone which has in its turn been faced with a brick frontage.

Although accurate dating is impossible, it is feasible to place brickwork in a relative chronology. A technique known as 'English bond' was especially popular in the sixteenth century and 'Flemish bond' in the eighteenth century. The colour of the bricks depends much on local conditions, but generally speaking the earliest bricks are a light pinkish-grey in colour. Tudor bricks, although found in many colours, produce an overall rich red effect, while seventeenth-century bricks are rich red and smooth in texture. Differences in the colour of bricks and mortar often betrays an alteration or addition to the fabric, even when the new work has been carefully bonded in, as older bricks tend to be smaller and more irregular in shape. In 1770 a minimum size was imposed by law and in 1784 a tax was levied on each brick; the building trade responded with larger bricks and gradually the present standard of three inches by four inches by ten inches was established. If timber is the predominant building material, attention should be paid to any evidence of exterior carving or jettying (an overhanging upper storey). Such features often imply wealth or pretensions on behalf of the builder, trying to create a structure of urban and therefore fashionable character.

External irregularities will often indicate that a building is old. A curving outline, for instance, often betrays a timber-framed or cob walled building. Similarly a house which appears to be either one-and-a-half or two-and-a-half storeys rather than a regular two- or three-storey structure should be examined in more detail. It may have been a medieval hall, which was originally open to the roof but later had an upper floor inserted. The next feature to examine is the chimney. A large stack built of rubble masonry at the end of a building or along the back is normally the sign of an old house. Similarly a large central chimney often indicates a more ancient structure. The dominant roofing material in the village should also be surveyed. Up until the eighteenth century roofing material was highly localized – thatch, slate and tile – but after the

XX An aerial view of the shifted settlement at Braybrooke, Leicestershire. The earthworks are centred on a former castle site, but there are extensive traces of buildings and tenement plots. It is interesting to note how ridge-and-furrow appears to have encroached upon an area of the abandoned settlement.

XXI The shrunken village of Ludborough, South Humberside. The earthworks reflect the pattern of rectangular tofts common on clayland sites. A string of dry fishponds can be seen at the top of the photograph together with traces of ploughed-out ridge-and-furrow. Note how the modern road bypasses the core of the ancient village resulting in more recent piecemeal development along its length.

XXII Vertical aerial view of Longnor, Staffordshire, showing the detailed topography of a small nucleated community – note the important role played by the roads and tracks in the village form. In the the centre of the village the market place has been encroached upon. The slight curve in the fields in the upper part of the picture indicates that they have been enclosed out of the open fields – and may have originally been laid out according to sun division.

XXIII Monington on Wye.

XXIV   Clun, Shropshire. A medieval borough, now the size of a small Midland village. The ancient settlement was based on the church (bottom), while the later town was planted in an extended eastern bailey of the castle. The new town was originally sited on wasteland.

XXV   North Cadeby, Lincolnshire. The earthworks of a deserted village in the process of gradually being eroded by ploughing.

XXVI The deserted village of Upper Chalford, Oxfordshire. The site lies in the Glyme valley in the Cotswolds and is one of a series of deserted medieval settlements occupying the steep unploughed valley slopes between Enstone and Chipping Norton.

beginning of the railway age, red bricks and Welsh slate were universally available and are found throughout the country.

What was the function of the building? Most of the buildings would of course have been dwelling houses but some of them would have had specialist functions. Particular attention should be paid to the farms within the village, whether redundant or operational. Often the presence of farm buildings, such as barns or stables, will suggest the position of former farms, which are now used as ordinary houses. Sometimes the demesne or manor farm will still be clearly identifiable, either from its site close to a large house or through its name. In communities where working farms are still located it is important to try and find out the location of the farm lands.

Other specialist buildings include the mill, inns and smithies; in many villages the cornmill has been converted to a house, and the blacksmith's into a garage. The former mill can be identified, firstly by its situation near a stream, often with its overgrown mill ponds and leats, and sometimes by the survival of a watermill or internal grinding machinery. The mill is also likely to be taller than other buildings in the village because it originally housed machinery and stored grain. The site of an inn was often chosen with care at a crossroads or on a market square and can therefore indicate an original focus within a settlement; thus it is important to locate former inns as well as those still functioning. In the cloth-making areas of the north, weavers' cottages are distinguished by wide first-floor windows which allowed plenty of light into the rooms. In Wiltshire they can be identified by the well-lit sheds at the back or side of the cottages. In the valley bottoms stand the mills which represent the first stage in the journey of the cloth industry back to the towns. The weavers' cottages belong to the sixteenth and seventeenth centuries, and the cloth mill and its retinue of terraced houses are familiar features in south Cotswold villages. Similar buildings can be identified in the villages of east Leicestershire where the hosiery industry developed in the eighteenth century.

In most rural settlements there are few public buildings, sometimes a row of sixteenth- or seventeenth-century almshouses will relate the charity of a prosperous local landowner. Many villages possess a school, but only rarely will this be much earlier than 1800. Many of these now lie derelict or have been converted into dwellings. The siting of the school may be of some interest. Sometimes it has been placed right outside the village, in other places it occupies a prominent position, close to the church as a result of an endowment by a philanthropic squire.

Other buildings to be found within the village will vary according to its geographical location and size. Larger villages will have many buildings associated with towns. For instance Fig. 20 shows that in the nineteenth century Lavenham (Suffolk) had not only the traditional village features – the parish church, rectory, windmill and hall, but also a railway station, library and factories and a corporate gasworks.

Fieldwork and deserted settlements

Although many deserted villages have received archaeological attention, most of the work has been on a relatively small scale and up to the present time no single village has been completely excavated. Indeed on many village sites work has taken place on only a single house area, and it is to be hoped that in the future more large-scale excavations can be undertaken in order that settlements may be seen in their entirety. In the circumstances, considerable emphasis must then be placed upon the value of fieldwork on deserted sites, for in most cases the field evidence will provide the only basis for study. The examination of the distribution, extent and types of deserted village earthworks can be of considerable value in interpreting settlement history, quite apart from aiding the understanding of an individual lost community. The techniques described here were developed largely with abandoned medieval villages and hamlets in mind, as they form by far the largest category of identified settlement earthwork sites. However, a growing number of Saxon, Romano-British and prehistoric settlement sites are coming to light and the fieldwork techniques are equally applicable to these.

The form of deserted settlement varies enormously. Some have substantial and easily recognizable earthworks, while others consist of no more than vague irregularities on the ground surface. On some there are no surface traces of the underlying site, perhaps because the earthworks have been ploughed, levelled or built upon. For our purposes those sites which have been destroyed are less important, although their location should be traced in order to provide as complete a picture of past settlement patterns as possible within any particular region. Basically the process is one of reconstructing the medieval settlement pattern, when villages and hamlets were at their most numerous throughout most of Britain.

In areas where little is known about the settlement pattern one of the easiest ways to begin the identification of the deserted sites is by locating isolated churches. If the church is of any antiquity and is also a parochial centre then almost certainly it would originally have served a larger nucleated community. There are, of course, exceptions to this pattern; many isolated churches in East Anglia appear to have sat by themselves since their construction; similarly there are dotted around the coasts of south-west Britain churches lying far away from any habitation – these were sited to serve itinerant fishermen and were not associated with a settled community. But in those instances where there was once a village why should the church remain when the rest of the village has moved or decayed? The church may have been the only stone structure in the old village and therefore was more likely to survive, and often after a village has been abandoned the church continued to serve the dispersed rural community and it carried with it a living and glebe-lands. The rector would still be in receipt of tithes from agriculturally productive land within the parish, which meant there was a vested interest in the survival of the church and its living.

All questions asked about the siting of a church and its fabric within an extant settlement are relevant to churches in deserted villages. It is necessary to visit the church and see if there are any associated earthworks in the surrounding fields, but the absence of clear earthworks need not deter the fieldworker. It should be noted if the church is served by a number of trackways or sunken roads, or whether the pattern of fields around the church differs from that in the rest of the parish. If there is a collection of relatively small enclosures they could represent former tenement plots, perhaps amalgamated into slightly larger units or possibly they might be the remains of old enclosures. The process of piecemeal enclosure often began on the strips lying adjacent to a settlement. A newly hedged field made up of a small bundle of strips carefully gathered by one man and then released from the communal open field by general agreement can often survive as a small enclosure today. Recent attempts at hedge dating have helped with the elucidation of problems such as this.

A particularly good example of an isolated church is provided by St Mary and St David, Kilpeck (Hereford & Worcester). This is one of the best small late Romanesque churches in Britain, built, it is believed, under the influence of the Hereford School of architects, working in the later part of the twelfth century. Quite apart from the remarkable church building, there are the remains and earthworks of a small Benedictine abbey to the south of the church, and the larger earthworks can be seen to the north-east, which appear to represent the defended village or small town of Kilpeck. These are in the shape of a roughly rectangular enclosure, about 100 metres by 70 metres, which is demarcated for much of its length by a scarp with traces of a rampart surviving in places. Along the axis of the enclosure runs a hollow-way which joins a metalled road at the northern end. This old road leads directly to the church, and offset from it there are a series of smaller enclosures, marking property boundaries and house platforms. The south-western corner of the large enclosure is occupied by a surviving farmhouse.

Fig. 32 shows the earthworks of the former village of Whitchurch (Warwicks); the churchyard appears to be later than the earthworks and fits rather uncomfortably into the earthwork pattern. The sunken way leading from the fishpond to the village is, however, partly respected by the northern churchyard boundary. Probably the best starting point for the location of isolated churches is the 1 : 50,000 OS map. It is normally possible to distinguish parish churches from nonconformist chapels and to determine if they are or have been parochial centres. It is then a fairly simple job to visit

180

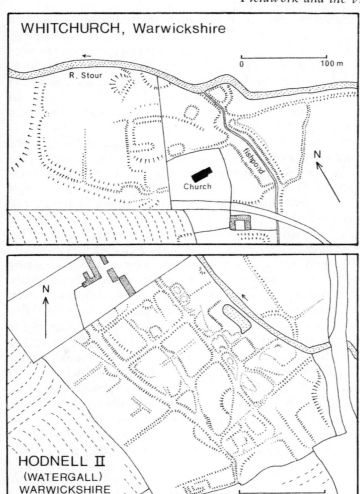

32. Earthwork plans of two deserted villages in Warwickshire. Hodnell was depopulated by the fifteenth century. By the end of the sixteenth century the church was in ruins and the whole parish enclosed and converted to pasture. At Whitchurch the church with some eleventh- and twelfth-century work survives. Sir Edward Belknap did much enclosing, causing depopulation in the time of Henry VII, and his successor put the manor house and a hundred acres of arable out of use. The chief centre of the settlement moved to Wimpstone, half a mile west of the church.

181

each church in turn to see whether there are any associated archaeological features. Within close proximity to Kilpeck, for instance, there are a considerable number of completely or nearly isolated churches (Fig. 33). Many of these such as St Devereux are surrounded by earthworks. In some cases such as Peterstow, the church is isolated, but a community has survived a little to the south on the line of the main Ross-Hereford road.

Another way of identifying deserted villages on the ground is by locating farmhouses which are of some antiquity or which possess authentic medieval place-names. The same procedure should be adopted as with the church: visit the site and try to determine the nature of any earthworks attached to the farm or old building. In the case of Great Oxenbold (Salop), for example, which was the site of a small house of the priors of Wenlock, a thirteenth-century chapel survives with three blocked lancet windows and the west is a hall containing sixteenth-century features. In the fields around there is a considerable area of earthworks indicating the presence of an early medieval community. It should be appreciated, however, that the buildings of a modern farm are often of sufficient size to completely mask any earthworks. In such cases surviving farm buildings should be examined for traces of ancient timber contained within later stone or brick encasements; in some instances old village houses have been incorporated into outbuildings of the surviving farm. At Siberscott (Salop), a fine late Tudor half-timbered farmhouse lies on the site of an earlier farm, but the outlying farmyard buildings incorporate the cruck trusses of an earlier medieval dwelling, which originally formed part of a small nucleated hamlet.

If there is an obvious source of local building material old quarries can often be found close to the site of the former community and in some instances quarrying has taken place on the actual site after the village was abandoned. This results in a confusion of earthworks which are difficult to interpret. Excavation at Detton Hall (Salop) revealed that apparently respectable earthworks representing house platforms and property boundaries, were the result of post-medieval marl

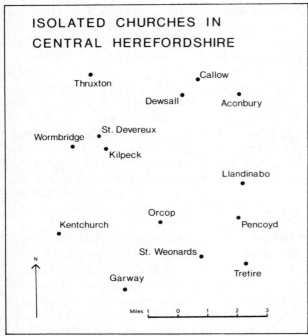

ISOLATED CHURCHES IN
CENTRAL HEREFORDSHIRE

Callow

Thruxton

Dewsall
Aconbury

St. Devereux

Wormbridge
Kilpeck

Llandinabo

Orcop

Kentchurch
Pencoyd

St. Weonards

N

Tretire

Garway

Miles 1   0   1   2   3

33. Plan of isolated churches in central Hereford.

quarrying, which by coincidence had taken place on the site of
deserted settlement.

Deserted medieval villages may also be identified through
field-names and other place-names. These can be traced from
the earliest surviving maps of the area and may well reveal the
presence of field-names such as 'Old Town Piece' indicating
the presence of a former settlement, or 'Black-lands' which
may indicate the debris from underlying occupation layers
finding its way to the surface and discolouring the soil. This
need not be a medieval site or even an area of former occupation such a feature may be caused by old industrial workings,
but it certainly provides a clue worth pursuing. Names such as
'Pavement Field' and 'Street Acre' may also provide evidence
of the presence of archaeological material.

A wide range of documentary sources may be used to
investigate former settlement sites. Such sources often indi-

183

cate only the existence of a site and in order to determine the precise location of the village it is necessary to undertake detailed fieldwork. Estate maps, plans and even early large-scale OS maps can reveal the whereabouts of the settlement. The development of local cartography in the late sixteenth century was just in time to capture the sites of many villages not long after they had been abandoned. A map of 1586 depicting the deserted village of Watborough (Leics) quite simply states 'the place where the towne of Whateborough stood'. The open-field strips depicted on the map are today visible in the form of ridge-and-furrow, and in many cases where the village has moved its site will be recorded with the prefix 'old' on early maps. Such as the site of 'Old Wheatley' (Oxon) depicted on a late sixteenth-century map of the All Souls College estate (Figs 34 and 35).

In some cases where there are extensive areas of ridge-and-furrow, the identification of blank spots may lead to the discovery of the villages. A typical example of this is Martinsthorpe (Leics, formerly Rutland), where almost the entire parish is covered with ridge-and-furrow and the village site stands out as a blank area. Where the earthworks have been levelled or ploughed away the village can normally only be identified when the soil has been ploughed. Indications of any underlying site may be found in the form of pottery or other artefacts, or through the presence of burnt clay, stone or brick. Distinctive soilmarks may aid identification: at Knighton on Teme (Worcs) traces of the village lie around the isolated church; only a few imprecise earthworks can be identified, but recent ploughing has resulted in a pattern of trackways to show up as dark linear features and the site of buildings to show as stone spreads and areas of burnt clay.

The identification of pottery scatters is being increasingly used as a technique for identifying former settlement sites. It has been used to particularly good effect in a group of parishes in East Anglia to trace the evolution of certain villages. In the case of Longham (Norfolk) a spread of mid and late Saxon pottery around the now isolated church indicates the area of early occupation. Medieval pottery was found in large quantities around the area of a green, which appears to have been

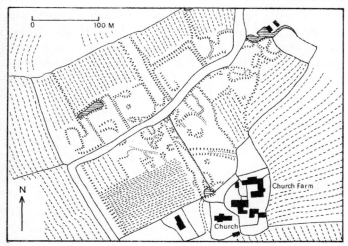

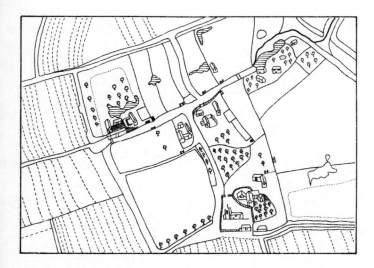

34. Grafton Flyford, Worcestershire. The plan of *c*.1770 (*bottom*) shows a settlement in the process of decay and can be compared to the resulting earthworks on the top plan after the village had disappeared. It is possible to identify common features such as the north-south road which has disappeared but is recognizable as a hollow way.

created in the twelfth century; in the post-medieval period the settlement appears to have shifted again to the edge of Kirtling Common (see Fig. 18). Thus on the basis of detailed field and cartographic analysis it is possible to detect two distinct phases of village movement and account for the dispersed settlement pattern visible today in the area.

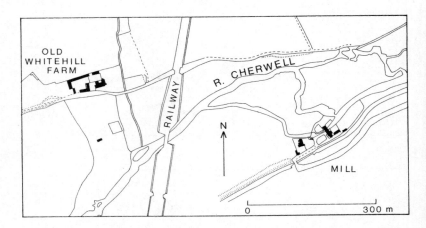

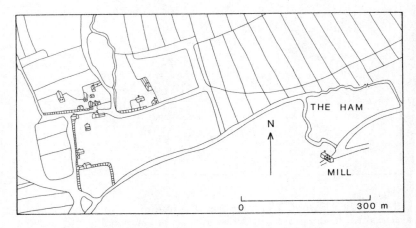

35. Whitehill deserted village, Oxfordshire. The map of 1608 shows the village still in existence, but it appears to have disappeared quickly after Parliamentary enclosure in 1795.

A convenient short cut, although not a substitute to field-walking, is provided by aerial photography. The camera, looking at the landscape from a vantage point, can identify irregularities in the ground surface which may not be immediately obvious on the ground and many villages and shrunken sites have thus been located. Sometimes the earth-works revealed by aerial photography are obscure but in others the village will be laid out like a map. A good example can be seen at Cestersover (Warwicks) where it has been possible to produce a plan based on the evidence from aerial photographs (Fig. 36). The high street can be clearly identified together with the various crofts and tofts which lie at right angles to the road. A precinct boundary can be identified marking the edge of the village and extensive ridge-and-furrow can also be clearly seen. On the western side it is possible to see how a croft boundary has been extended across the ridge-and-furrow, perhaps during a period of village expansion. The different alignment of the roads and crofts in the northern part of the village suggests that this might have been the original settlement and that the southern limb was created at a subsequent stage. Such relationships between earthwork features are often best defined on aerial photo-graphs and can sometimes lead to a tentative interpretation of the chronology of the ground features. This plan also shows the medieval chapel situated amongst the modern farm build-ings, the moated manor house, and the fishpond to the west on the line of a former stream. Plate XXV shows the deserted medieval village of North Cadeby (Lincs) where there are also traces of settlement expansion over areas of former ridge-and-furrow. The earthworks in the field to the top left and top right of the main earthwork field have been ploughed out and the lines of roads are visible only as soil markings. There are indistinct traces of houses and other features although the ploughed-out ridge-and-furrow can be fairly easily identified. The road which once served the village now stops at the farmhouse outside the village earthworks.

Once a site has been located it is necessary to examine the earthworks and other physical features in order to try and understand the layout of the settlement. Reference has already

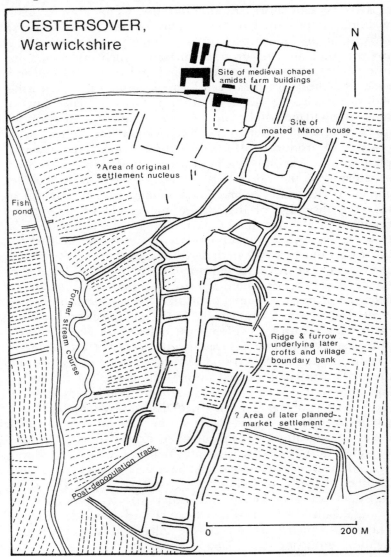

CESTERSOVER, Warwickshire

N ↑

Site of medieval chapel amidst farm buildings

Site of moated Manor house

?Area of original settlement nucleus

Fish pond

Former stream course

Ridge & furrow underlying later crofts and village boundary bank

? Area of later planned market settlement

Post-depopulation track

0   200 M

36. Cestersover, Warwickshire. Diagrammatic plan of a deserted village taken from an aerial photograph, showing the extension of the village over areas of former arable.

been made to the importance of the position of the church. Does it, for instance, lie easily within the village plan? Is it at some distance away from the earthwork, as in the case of Alvingham (Lincs) where the church obviously lay at the very end of the street, or is it completely divorced from the earthwork features? Frequently only detailed local study both of the ground and documentary evidence will elucidate the reasons for such movement.

The next feature we must look for is a manor house – this may occupy a larger plot in the earthwork plan or it may be distinguishable by the presence of a moat, but in many cases it will not be possible to identify a separate demesne area within the village earthworks. Attention should be paid to the shape of any larger earthworks to see if a house plan can be identified. Moated manor houses were sometimes constructed on deserted sites after they were abandoned and it is therefore necessary to see whether the boundaries of the manor house respect the earthworks of the deserted village. If they do not it may be possible to show that the house is subsequent to the village desertion.

Attention should then be paid to the actual shape of the village earthworks. We have already seen that castles, abbeys, churches and manor houses can all help fashion the shape of a village, but it is the subsidiary buildings with their tofts and crofts which make up the settlement network. The house platforms will tend to lie along the roads, sometimes flanking them, sometimes set on end. Between the buildings, which were seldom linked together as a single frontage, there were open spaces completing the width of the long narrow crofts at the head of which the house was commonly set. The crofts were sometimes long and narrow and had the appearance of open-field strips gathered at the back doors of houses. In some cases it looks as if villages were laid out in just such a way occupying these strips. In a simple village plan the length of the croft ran back from the house and reached back as far as the edge of the fields.

At the meeting place of croft and open-field strips there was often a back lane, a perimeter road giving access to the crofts. This was bounded on one side by a ditch and fence which kept domestic animals from straying into arable fields, and on the other by the croft hedges which helped to keep out predators. Here and there alley-ways led from the street to the back lane, running between the crofts. When the village earthworks show some crofts regular in length and direction flanked by others of irregular directions it is normally the sign that additions have been made to the original nucleus.

The best earthworks will have the appearance of a photographic negative of the former village and can often be reinforced in dry weather by parch marks, which show the actual sites of former houses and outbuildings. Such an example is West Firsby (Lincs), a stone site where a great complexity of buildings overlying each other can be identified. The worst can be indistinguishable from surface quarrying remains. If the buildings were of stone then the earthworks may have grown over the tumbled footings of the houses. In some cases stones may still be visible on the surface or poking through the grass, and recently abandoned areas may be characterized by the presence of shrubs and nettles growing over a newly formed soil horizon on top of the irregularly fallen rubble. At Nether Chalford (Oxon), for instance, the use of limestone has resulted in the survival of walls up to a metre in height and many of the entrances and internal divisions within the buildings can still be distinguished (Plate XXVI).

Earthworks can be deceptive in some cases. Deserted village earthworks may be confused with or in some cases associated with the surviving earthworks of castles, priories, ornamental gardens and mineral workings of varying kinds. At Osmington, West Ringstead (Dorset) the deserted village earthworks have been confused by a system of later sluices cut across them. The earthworks of the deserted site of Papley, Warmington parish (Northants) are even more misleading. On the ground they appear to represent a typical deserted medieval village; the documentation for the site implies such a settlement and records its depopulation in some detail. However, cartographic evidence indicates that with the possible exception of two or three house platforms, this is not the case. The development of the whole earthwork site can be explained in terms of post-medieval occupation comprising two successive

190

farmhouses, farm buildings with yards, approach roads and labourer cottages.

Where stone or brick were not used then the house earthworks are likely to be far less obvious. They may, however, appear as a negative area in a slightly sunken form indicating where the ground level has built up outside the timber walls or stone sills. In other cases they may have left no traces at all but the tofts or enclosures may be identified by the boundary banks where hedges or fences once stood. In clay areas the only boundaries may originally have been in the form of ditches and these may still be identifiable as such, often with a slight counter scarp indicating the up-cast from the frequent dredging that would have been necessary to keep water free flowing. In some cases property boundaries may still carry a hedge, a fence or wall and although this may not have been the original form of partition it will represent the fossilization of that boundary line in a later field or garden pattern.

The roads of the village will mostly be sunken ways, often flanked by the up-cast caused either in their original construction or as they work themselves down into the ground surface. The village streets will not normally have been paved or metalled in any way but occasionally traces of cobbling may be identified through parch marks.

Other features to look for are springs, wells, village ponds and field ponds and concentrations along the line of streams and rivers. The footings for mills can also often be identified close to streams and the leats feeding off the stream can be traced as straight lines cutting off meanders. In some areas it is possible to identify the sites of windmills. Their earthworks normally consist of a simple circular mound and ditch and are sometimes mistaken for a prehistoric burial mound. Many deserted and extant villages have traces of fishponds. The popular belief is that fish breeding was exclusively associated with monasteries and their properties, but fishponds are to be found in a large number of villages with no monastic associations. They provided fish which augmented the meat diet and it is evident that villagers as well as manorial householders drew from them. The earthworks of fishponds are sometimes mistaken for moats but they can normally be distinguished

191

without much difficulty. Fishponds are rectangular excavations beside a small stream or near a spring, and are not usually set in the course of larger streams or rivers. Embankments were used to maintain a pool of moderate depth with a gentle flow of water through it, as a large stream would break down the banks in time of flood and sweep the fish away.

The pond was often made by building an earthen dam across the line for the water course. One side of this bank may have been stone faced for rigidity while a sluice served as a safety valve in wet weather. In normal times there would be a slight flow over the lip of the sluice. If the valley sides were not themselves sufficiently steep, two further embankments might have been constructed parallel to the stream, with a possible fourth bank higher than the pond to complete the rectangle. Today these earthworks do not normally retain water as the dams have been breached and the pond may be completely dry if modern field drainage or piped water supplies have siphoned the water away. In their developed form fishponds had auxiliary breeding chambers linked to them by a system of channels and sluices; it seems probable that different chambers were for different types of fish. Altogether the fishponds with their adjuncts can cover a considerable area or length of valley.

The settlement earthworks will not explain why or when the settlement was abandoned, nor the detailed history of the site prior to its desertion: such answers can be provided only by excavation and documentary research. The earthworks represent the process of decay and erosion of the village fabric after it has been abandoned. Quite clearly most villages were not completely abandoned at the one time and individual settlements often decayed over a considerable period of time; nonetheless the earthworks will provide a clue to the layout of the former community and in some cases an explicit village plan may be revealed; and careful fieldwork can identify phases of settlement expansion and contraction.

Conclusion

It should be stressed that no single manual, even less a single chapter, can guide the fieldworker to the total understanding of the village past and present. The fieldworker should acquaint himself with the area which he wishes to examine to understand the building styles, economic activities and perhaps most important of all, the local idiosyncrasies which characterize so many English settlements. It is, however, essential that the fieldworker should try to absorb all forms of visible information, and should be ready to incorporate all other information, including folk memory, which, if used cautiously, can be of considerable assistance. We are trying to understand the morphology of the village – how and why it looks as it does. This involves total awareness of all the surviving forms of evidence.

SELECT BIBLIOGRAPHY

Anderson, M. D., *History and Imagery in British Churches* (1971).

Aston, M. and Rowley, T., *Landscape Archaeology* (1974).

Beresford, M. W., *History on the Ground* (1957).

Brunskill, R. W., *Illustrated Handbook of Vernacular Architecture* (1971).

Clifton-Taylor, A., *The Pattern of English Building* (1972).

Field, H., *English Field-Names* (1972).

Fowler, P. J. (ed.), *Recent Work in Rural Archaeology* (1975).

Harvey, N., *A History of Farm Buildings in England and Wales* (1970).

Ordnance Survey, *Field Archaeology in Great Britain* (Fifth ed., 1973).

Smith, J. T. and Yates, E. M., 'On the Dating of English Houses from External Evidence', reprinted from *Field Studies*, Vol. 2, No. 5 (1968).

Taylor, C., *Fieldwork in Medieval Archaeology* (1974).

West, J., *Village Records* (1962).

Appendix 1

COMMITTEE for RESCUE ARCHAEOLOGY in AVON, GLOUCESTERSHIRE and SOMERSET VILLAGES SURVEY

_____ DISTRICT

Hundred	name of settlement	parish (unless the same)	NGR

NATURE OF SETTLEMENT

Village	Hamlet	Farm	House

GEOLOGY   SOILS

Map No.   Map No.

Nearest Water Supply

General Description of plan type

Church Dedication

Church: plan type, architecture
and topography

Topography

Listed buildings and notes on others of interest

Archaeological Records (os)

194

AIR PHOTOGRAPHS

Numbers:

Tracing:

Figure 1a Pro-forma (front)

Specific Bibliography

Place-Name

Anglo-Saxon Document

Domesday Book

VCH information/Collinson

Pre-19th century map

Tracing

Tithe Map

Tracing

PLANNING INFORMATION

Present condition

Long-term planning policy

---

1. Housing   Map

---

2. Services   Map

Recommendation

Figure 1b. Pro-forma (rear)

Appendix 2

Isle Abbotts (Fig. 37)

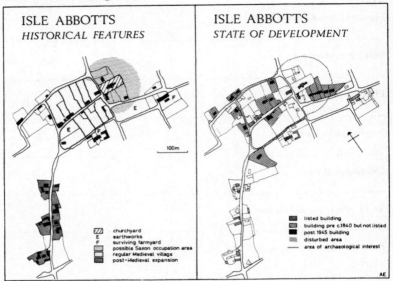

ISLE ABBOTTS
HISTORICAL FEATURES

ISLE ABBOTTS
STATE OF DEVELOPMENT

100m

churchyard
E earthworks
F surviving farmyard
possible Saxon occupation area
regular Medieval village
post-Medieval expansion

listed building
building pre c.1840 but not listed
post 1945 building
disturbed area
area of archaeological interest

37. Rapid survey plans of Isle Abbotts, Somerset, to assess archaeological and historical importance.

CONVENTIONAL HISTORY

1.1   Isle Abbotts is named after the River Isle which separates the parish from the neighbouring one of Isle Brewers. Isle is a Celtic river-name which was first mentioned as *Yle* in a Saxon charter of AD 693 (Ekwall 1936). The second element of the place-name indicates that the village was owned by a monastic foundation during the medieval period. Domesday Book records that by 1086 the manor was in fact one of the holdings of Muchelney Abbey, situated three miles to the north-east, although it may not have belonged to the abbey in the time of Edward (VCH, Somerset, I, 468). The manor was held by Muchelney until the dissolution in 1538, when it passed to the Earl of Hertford, along with the abbey itself (Collinson 1791, I, 50–1).

196

THE CHURCH

2.1 The fabric of St. Mary's church is mainly Perpendicular, although the chancel dates from *c.* 1300 and the north aisle was added in the early sixteenth century (Pevsner 1958, 205–7; Wickham 1965). The elaborate detailing, which includes one of the finest Somerset towers with statues contained in decorated niches, internal panelled arches, a sedilia and carved piscina, reflects the monastic ownership of the village during the medieval period.

2.2 The presence of a Norman font (reworked in the Gothic style) within the church suggests the existence of a pre-fourteenth-century church, although this may not necessarily have occupied the same site as the surviving building. The present church, however, stands on a small island of land above the level of the rest of the village (G.A.A. MS) and this island may well have formed the nucleus of the Saxon village, if not the site of the pre-fourteenth-century church.

DOMESTIC BUILDINGS

3.1 There are several large cottages probably dating from the sixteenth and seventeenth centuries. They mainly cluster near the church and are in good condition.

TOPOGRAPHY

4.1 The surviving village incorporates two elements; a central regular area and an irregular, linear extension. The regular area was probably laid out in the medieval period while the linear extension is likely to be post-medieval in origin.

4.2 The regular area comprises two rows of rectangular properties stretching back at right angles from the main village street to a pair of parallel back lanes. These back lanes survive today as hollow ways. The boundaries surviving in the nineteenth century suggest that there may originally have been six properties each side of the street. The main village street is aligned on the church. However, whether the medieval church was laid out at the same time as the village street or whether the main street was aligned on an existing church building cannot be ascertained from the topographical evidence. The siting of the church on a slightly raised island may suggest that the church has always occupied the same spot (see above) and this might indicate that the village plan was laid out with reference to the site of the existing church.

4.3   The date of the laying out of the regular village plan is unknown. If it took place in the middle or later medieval period, then it presumably replaced the former layout of the earlier Saxon/ early medieval settlement. If this is the case it can be postulated that the Saxon village may have occupied part of the area later covered by the planned village and the land immediately adjacent to the church.

4.4   In addition to the regular area of the village there are two homesteads probably dating from the late medieval period which are located immediately outside the limits of the regular village. Both survive today as working farms.

4.5   The second main element of the village plan is a linear extension of the settlement along the road leading south-west from the village nucleus. The surviving buildings, which include the Non-Conformist Chapel (Bethesda, 1805), and the narrow irregular properties suggest that this expansion took the form of a series of encroachments during the post-medieval period.

SURVIVING EARTHWORKS

5.1   Within the regular village area, only six of the postulated twelve original properties were occupied by buildings in the early nineteenth century. However, surviving earthworks in the western sector of the regular area suggest that homesteads were originally present in each rectangular land unit. The earthworks clearly indicated the presence of house platforms fronting the main village street. The banks survive to a height of 1.0–1.5 metres and are of great archaeological importance.

5.2   Vague low earthworks are also present in the orchard south of the church in an area where previous medieval and possibly Saxon settlement are to be expected.

PRESENT CONDITION

6.1   The village is well kept and the focus on the magnificent church and the main street of the regular village survives well. In the long term a certain amount of infilling may be allowed and a good deal of modern (post-1945) building has already taken place in the village. This includes eight dwellings within the regular village area and several more just outside it.

6.2   In some cases the modern dwellings have been inserted into surviving property units and facing the main street, but one has been built in the rear half of a unit fronting on to one of the back lanes while, south of the church, a row of houses has been erected with no reference to the previous property boundaries.

198

Recommendations

TOPOGRAPHY

7.1   The surviving boundary lines between the properties in the main part of the village reflect the pattern of land units laid out in the medieval period and should therefore be respected wherever possible. This can best be achieved by building new dwellings within the boundaries of existing units and by facing the new buildings on to the old main streets.

7.2   If there is a choice between locating new dwellings in the regular village nucleus, in the late village extension or elsewhere, then, on archaeological grounds, the last location would be preferable.

EARTHWORKS

7.3   The earthworks at the western end of the village are very well preserved and form an integral element of the regular village dating at least from the medieval period. This site is of great archaeological importance within the village and should be designated as an open space in a future local plan. If, however, for other compelling reasons, development of this field cannot be avoided, then provision should be made for a full archaeological investigation involving survey and detailed excavation prior to development. Adequate financial provision would be required to ensure that these investigations could be carried out to the highest archaeological standards.

7.4   The orchard south of the church contains slight earthworks in an area where medieval and possibly Saxon settlement are to be expected. Any development in this field would need to be preceded by a detailed archaeological survey and the construction would have, at the least, to be watched by a trained archaeologist in order that any evidence relating to earlier occupation could be recorded.

References

Collinson 1791 Collinson, J., *History of Somerset* (3 volumes, 1791).

Ekwall 1936 Ekwall, E., *Concise Oxford Dictionary of English Place-Names* (1936).

G.A.A. MS., *Isle Abbots*. Somerset Archaeological and Natural History Society Library, Taunton Castle (undated).

Pevsner 1958 Pevsner, N., *South and West Somerset* (1958).

Wickham 1965 Wickham A. K., *Churches of Somerset* (1965).

Bibliography

There is very little literature that deals with the village 'in the round', but there are an increasing number of specialist studies, examining the village from the viewpoint of the archaeologist, historian, planner and sociologist. Apart from papers and monographs covering individual settlements or groups of settlements, the most useful topographical studies are the recent volumes of the Royal Commission on Historical Monuments, and the county books in the *Making of the English Landscape* series.

Allison, K. J., *The East Riding of Yorkshire Landscape* (1976).

Allerston, P., 'English Village Development', *Transactions of the Institute of British Geographers*, 51 (1970).

Aston, M. and Rowley, T., *Landscape Archaeology* (1974).

Baker, R. H. and Harley, J. B., *Man Made the Land* (1973).

Beresford, M. W., *History on the Ground* (1957).

Beresford, M. W. and St Joseph, K. J. S., *Medieval England: An aerial survey* (1957).

Beresford, M. W. and Hurst, J. G. (eds), *Deserted Medieval Villages* (1971).

Bonham-Carter, V., *The English Village* (1952).

Brandon, P., *The Sussex Landscape* (1974).

Cameron, K., *English Place-Names* (1961).

Chisholm, M., *Rural Settlement and Land Use* (second revised ed., 1968).

Darby, H. C. (ed.), *A New Historical Geography of England* (1973).

Darley, G., *Villages of Vision* (1975).

Emery, F., *The Oxfordshire Landscape* (1974).

Finberg, H. P. R., *The Gloucestershire Landscape* (new ed., 1975).

Finberg, H. P. R., *Roman and Saxon Withington* (1965).

Finberg, J., *Exploring Villages* (1958).

Hallam, S. J., 'Villages in Roman Britain': Some evidence, *The Antiquaries Journal*, 44 (1964).

Homans, G. C., *English Villagers of the Thirteenth Century* (1960).

Hoskins, W. G., *The Making of the English Landscape* (1955).

Jones, G. R. J., 'Settlement Patterns in Anglo-Saxon England', *Antiquity*, 35 (1961).

Jones, G. R. J., 'Basic Patterns of Settlement Distribution in Northern England', *Advancement of Science*, 71 (1961).

Maitland, F. W., *Domesday Book and Beyond* (1897).

Mills, D. R., *The English Village* (1968).

Munby, L., *The Hertfordshire Landscape* (1977).

Newton, R., *The Northumberland Landscape* (1972).

Palliser, D. M., *The Staffordshire Landscape* (1976).

Raistrick, A., *West Riding of Yorkshire* (1970).

Roberts, B. K., 'The Study of Village Plans', *The Local Historian*, 9, No. 15 (1971).

Roberts, B. K., *Rural Settlement in Britain* (1977).

Rowley, T., *The Shropshire Landscape* (1972).

Royal Commission on Historical Monuments (England), *Cambridgeshire*, Vols I and II (1968 and 1972).

R.C.H.M. (England), *Archaeological Sites in North-East Northamptonshire* (1975).

R.C.H.M. (England), *County of Dorset*, Vols 2 *South-East* (1970), 3 *Central* (1970), 4 *North* (1972), 5 *East* (1975).

R.C.H.M. (England), *County of Gloucester*, Vol. 1 *Iron Age and Romano-British Cotswolds* (1976).

R.C.H.M. (England), *Shielings and Bastles* (1970).

Sawyer, P. H. (ed.), *Medieval Settlement* (1976).

Scarfe, N., *The Suffolk Landscape* (1972).

Seebohm, F., *The English Village Community* (1890).

Sharp, T., *The Anatomy of the Village* (1946).

Steane, J., *The Northamptonshire Landscape* (1974).

Taylor, C., *The Cambridgeshire Landscape* (1973).

Taylor, C., *Dorset* (1970).

Thomas, A. C. (ed.), *Rural Settlements in Roman Britain* (1966).

Williams, M., *The South Wales Landscape* (1975).

Yates, E. M., 'A Study of Settlement Patterns', *Field Studies*, 1 No. 3 (1961).

Index

205